TEENS PARENTING
YOUR PREGNANCY
AND NEWBORN JOURNEY

Other Books by Jeanne Warren Lindsay:

Teens Parenting—Your Baby's First Year
Teens Parenting—The Challenge of Toddlers
Teen Dads: Rights, Responsibilities and Joys
Do I Have a Daddy? A Story About a Single-Parent Child
School-Age Parents: Challenge of Three-Generation Living
Teenage Marriage: Coping with Reality
Teens Look at Marriage: Rainbows, Roles and Reality
Parents, Pregnant Teens and the Adoption Option
Pregnant Too Soon: Adoption Is an Option
Open Adoption: A Caring Option

By Jeanne Lindsay and Jeanne Brunelli
Translated by Argentina Palacios
Adolescentes como padres—La jornada de tu embarazo
y el nacimiento de tu bebé

By Jeanne Lindsay and Sally McCullough
Teens Parenting—Discipline from Birth to Three

By Jeanne Lindsay and Sharon Rodine:
Teen Pregnancy Challenge, Book One:
Strategies for Change
Teen Pregnancy Challenge, Book Two:
Programs for Kids

By Jeanne Lindsay and Catherine Monserrat:
Adoption Awareness: Help for Teachers,
Counselors, Nurses and Caring Others

TEENS PARENTING
YOUR PREGNANCY AND NEWBORN JOURNEY

How to Take Care of Yourself and Your Newborn If You're a Pregnant Teen

Jeanne Warren Lindsay, MA, CHE

and

Jean Brunelli, PHN

Morning Glory Press

Buena Park, California

Teens Parenting—Your Pregnancy and Newborn Journey
(Also available in Easier Reading and Spanish Editions)
is part of a four-book series. Other titles are:
Teens Parenting—Your Baby's First Year
Teens Parenting—The Challenge of Toddlers
Teens Parenting—Discipline from Birth to Three

Library of Congress Cataloging-in-Publication Data
Lindsay, Jeanne Warren.
Teens parenting-- your pregnancy and newborn journey: how to take
care of yourself and your newborn if you're a pregnant teen / Jeanne
Warren Lindsay and Jean Brunelli.
192 p.
Includes bibliographical references and index.
Summary: Discusses nutritional, medical, and social aspects of
teenage pregnancy and teenage parenthood.
ISBN 0-930934-51-2 : $15.95. -- ISBN 0-930934-50-4 (pbk.) :
$9.95
1. Prenatal care. 2. Teenage pregnancy. 3. Teenage parents.
[1. Pregnancy. 2. Teenage parents.] I. Brunelli, Jean. II. Title.
RG556.5.L56 1991
618.2'4--dc20   91-3712
                                                        CIP
                                                         AC

MORNING GLORY PRESS, INC.
6595 San Haroldo Way   Buena Park, CA 90620-3748
(714) 828-1998
Printed and bound in the United States of America

Contents

ACKNOWLEDGMENTS

We are grateful to Robert Blum, Mary Crowley, Ann Nation, Julie Vetica, Sue Manzo, Anita Gallegos, Marilyn Lanphier, and Joan Stringer who made time to read and critique our manuscript. Their comments were invaluable.

Perhaps even more important is the input from pregnant and parenting teens, the young people we interviewed, and whose wisdom is scattered throughout the book. Sixty-one young people are quoted, and many of them gave us permission to include their names.

They include Molina Lopez, David Munoz, Meisha Washington, Anita Smith, Tammy Miller, Jessica Aguilar, Jennifer Launchbury, Maria Espinoza, Holly Buchanan, Michelle Conway, Michelle Balderrama, Dora Alves, Selena Diaz, Terry Emerson, Angela Cardena, Larry Jaurequi, Lynetta Allen, Tammy Ayala, Christi Gifford, Karen Lind, Kaykeysha Blankenship, Harmony Gonzales, Pao Chen, Shawna Moreno, Roberto Guzman, Luby Ventura, Therese Albert, Linda Solano, Albert Aguilar, Maria Vasquez, Tammy Gutierrez, David Chang, Damion Phillips, Tracy Bradshaw, Santiago Sandoval, Ana Perez, David Lena. We interviewed others who are quoted and acknowledged in the other *Teens Parenting* series of books.

David Crawford, teacher in the Teen Mother Program, William Daylor High School, Sacramento, supplied most of the photographs. His models were his wonderful students. Barbara Hellstrom provided the illustrations.

Tim Rinker is the cover artist, and Steve Lindsay helped design the book. We appreciate so much the contributions of all of these talented people.

Carole Blum and Marlene Boehm again helped with the proof-reading and kept Morning Glory Press alive and well during book production time. Erin Lindsay helped with the typing and proof-reading. We thank them for their valuable support.

We're especially grateful to our ever-supportive spouses, Mike Brunelli and Bob Lindsay. We love them.

Jeanne Lindsay
Jean Brunelli

Preface

If you're going to have a baby, you're preparing for a wonderful and sometimes scary event. Your baby's healthy development depends to a great extent on what you do throughout your pregnancy. Your own health and well being depend on you taking good care of yourself during this important time.

This book is for you. It's not written for your teachers or your parents or for students in your school's health class. It's written directly to you, a pregnant teenager, and to your partner if you're still together.

Much of *Your Pregnancy and Newborn Journey* focuses on your pregnancy and on your labor and delivery. Your baby will become more and more real to you as the months go by, and how you care for yourself is extremely important to that small person inside you.

As you do all you can to help your baby develop well, remember that your needs continue to be extremely important. You're a teenager who happens to be pregnant. You have a lot of decisions to make and planning to do regarding your coming child. Don't forget your own needs as you do this planning.

We have both worked with hundreds of pregnant teenagers, and for this book we interviewed in depth many of these young women. We've also interviewed teenage fathers because we thought you'd be interested in their feelings on the subject of their fatherhood.

Actually, this book is co-authored not just by us, but also by these many young people who shared their experiences and their thoughts with us. As each young parent is quoted, s/he is identified by age, children, and children's ages. If the same parent is quoted again in the same chapter, only her/his name is listed. Names have been changed, but the quotes and the ages given are always real.

These young parents discuss their reasons for eating nutritious foods and staying away from alcohol, drugs, and smoking during pregnancy. They share their labor and delivery stories. They talk about the stresses and the joys of caring for a newborn baby. You may find their comments more helpful than ours because these are your peers, young adults who have already experienced the things you're experiencing as a pregnant teen.

We wish you the best as you continue on your pregnancy and newborn journey—surely one of the most important journeys you will ever take.

Jeanne Lindsay
Jean Brunelli
April, 1991

Foreword

Nearly half a million adolescents have babies each year. Many of these young women do not realize the health risks involved in having a child at such a young age. They have undertaken the task of developing another human being while their own bodies are still developing.

A young mother is one and one-half times more likely to deliver a low-birthweight baby (less than 5 1/2 pounds). The birth of low-birthweight infants is associated with higher levels of inadequate prenatal care.

Low birthweight is a largely solvable problem. We know a great deal about what causes it, and how to prevent it. We know the importance of early and regular prenatal care, but we also know that almost half of all teenage mothers do not receive first trimester prenatal care.

Today we know the importance of detecting and preventing problems, life style, genetic, and environmental,
that can affect the baby at every stage of development.

I have been involved with pregnant adolescents through
the March of Dimes Birth Defects Foundation's interest in
the alarming statistics among babies delivered to teen
mothers, statistics concerning both low-birthweight and
birth defects. At the March of Dimes, our experience has
shown that the first step in preventing birth defects is to
minimize risk. The first step in minimizing risk is
education!

A pregnant teen who continues her education has a
decided advantage both physically and emotionally. Support in the school setting has proven to be a key factor in
improved pregnancy outcome. There, she becomes aware
of her responsibility in keeping prenatal care appointments
and maintaining a healthier diet. She learns how important
it is to avoid smoking, alcohol, and drugs because all are
added risks to her developing baby.

Jeanne Lindsay and Jean Brunelli's new book will be an
important tool in education. As usual, Jeanne's interviews
with pregnant and parenting teens are lessons in reality.

Working with hundreds of teen mothers over the past
nineteen years has given Jeanne and Jean insight in and
sensitivity to the needs of this special population.

Life's most important journey is usually a stunning
success—*if* the baby's parents are making healthy choices
to achieve this goal. *Teens Parenting—Your Pregnancy
and Newborn Journey* is a very special, readable, and
practical book.

Anita A. Gallegos
Former Director, Community Services
March of Dimes Birth Defects Foundation
Southern California Chapter

To our students

who helped us develop the knowledge

we share here

She's already parenting her unborn child.

CHAPTER 1

PARENTING STARTS WITH PREGNANCY

I was real sad because I couldn't believe I was pregnant—and I didn't want to believe it. But as the days and months went by and I got bigger and bigger, I finally had to face it. I had to move on to the next step.

My parents were hurt, but they stuck by me and helped me deal with the situation.

Elysha, pregnant at 17

This book is about pregnancy. It's also about parenting because parenting begins at conception. How you take care of yourself while you're pregnant is an extremely important part of parenting.

What you do now has a great deal to do with your baby becoming a mentally and physically healthy human being. If you see your doctor regularly, eat the "right" foods, and avoid alcohol, tobacco, and drugs, you're being a "good" parent long before you can hold your baby in your arms.

A baby can be most damaged during the first two months of pregnancy. Many women don't see a doctor and may not know they're pregnant during this important time.

Since you're reading this book, you've probably already verified your pregnancy. You and your partner may be pleased and excited about your coming baby. Perhaps your family is supportive, too.

Your Feelings Matter

How are you feeling about yourself? Some teens are excited about being pregnant. Having a new life growing inside you can be exciting. If this pregnancy came as a shock to you, however, you may be feeling pretty depressed about the whole thing.

> *I stopped going to my regular high school when I was three months pregnant. I didn't want anybody to know, so I didn't go anywhere. I think that made everything worse. I could have stayed at my regular high school and gone ahead with my activities, at least for awhile.*
>
> Maurine, pregnant at 14

You might want to read *Surviving Teen Pregnancy: Your Choices, Dreams, and Decisions* by Shirley Arthur (1991: Morning Glory Press). It's a practical guide to thinking through the decisions you must make and the steps you need to take to have the kind of life you want in spite of (or because of) your pregnancy.

Many pregnant teens are frightened and even a little desperate when they realize they're pregnant "too soon." If this is how you feel, you need to find help immediately.

See Your Doctor Early!

If you think you're pregnant, please see a doctor right away. Get your questions answered. You may be scared— the unknown is often *very* scary. Perhaps you don't know what to do. The best thing to do now is to find a clinic where you can get a pregnancy test.

As you probably realize by now, trying to pretend you aren't pregnant won't help anyone. Yet many young women, shocked at the idea of having conceived, ignore the whole thing—sometimes for several months.

> *I ignored the whole idea of pregnancy for six or seven months. I didn't tell my parents until right before I enrolled in the Teen Mother Program. I ignored it for the whole summer. My boyfriend had moved, so it was just me. He moved before I found out I was pregnant, so I didn't tell him. I think he still doesn't know.*
>
> Pati, pregnant at 16

Getting your pregnancy verified early is important for several reasons.

First, a lot of young women who don't want to be pregnant go through the agony of thinking they are, when, in fact, they aren't. If you aren't pregnant, you might as well find out. Then, if you don't want to be pregnant, you can do something so you don't conceive accidentally.

Second, you have more options if your pregnancy is verified early. If you consider having an abortion, you need to make your decision as soon as possible. An abortion performed very early in pregnancy, preferably during the first twelve weeks after conception, is easier on the woman both physically and mentally than is a later abortion. Seldom will an abortion be performed on a person who is more than twenty weeks pregnant.

For six months I didn't show, I didn't gain weight, and I just didn't think about it. I blocked it out of my mind. Then all of a sudden, I had an ultrasound done, and I was 26 weeks pregnant. Of course that was too far along to do anything except keep it. I didn't really realize I couldn't have an abortion until the counselor said, "Well, it's too late now."

Lucia, 16 - placed her baby for adoption

Third—and perhaps the most important reason for an early pregnancy test—is the need for early and regular prenatal care throughout pregnancy. If you're pregnant, you need to see your doctor right away.

If I had told my grandmother sooner, I probably would have gotten prenatal care. I think it would have helped me both mentally and physically. Hiding was hard. I was nervous, always tense, never wanted to come home because I didn't want them to see me. Everyone was getting the idea, and I wanted to be the one to tell my grandma.

I guess I waited so long because I was scared. I thought my boyfriend was going to be there through everything to help me, but he wasn't. It doesn't always work out the way you want it to.

Elisa Marie, pregnant at 14

Early prenatal care is essential for baby's as well as mother's health. Many of the problems teenagers face during pregnancy are the result of these young women not seeing their doctors until late in their pregnancies. Anyone who thinks she might be pregnant should be under a doctor's care at least by the time she's three months pregnant.

The doctor will check you carefully for any condition which might interfere with a healthy pregnancy. S/he will probably prescribe prenatal vitamins and recommend the kinds of foods you should be eating.

Medical Expenses of Pregnancy

Important as it is, medical care during pregnancy and delivery is expensive. A pregnant teenager may qualify for medical care under her family's health plan. Or she and/or her baby's father may have health insurance through her/his work.

In some states, if you don't have health insurance, you may be eligible for Medicaid. If you are, you can get prenatal health care at no charge to you or to your parents. To find out if this is available where you live, call your local Department of Public Social Services (welfare department).

Some areas have prenatal health clinics where women can get prenatal checkups at no charge—or they may be charged according to their income.

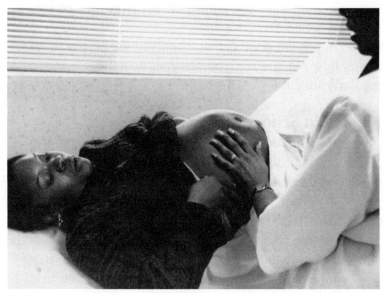

Let your doctor guide you to a safe and healthy delivery.

*Teenagers who don't get early medical care
are more likely to have serious
health problems themselves
during pregnancy.*

Many organizations such as the March of Dimes Birth
Defects Foundation are concerned about the poor outcome
of many teenage pregnancies. They know that teenagers
who do not get early medical care are more likely to have
serious health problems themselves during pregnancy.
They also know that babies born to teenage mothers may be
born too soon and be smaller than average. Premature, too-
small babies are more likely to have physical and mental
handicaps than are bigger, full-term babies.

For these reasons, the March of Dimes especially wants
to help pregnant teenagers get good prenatal care. If you
don't know where to go or how to pay for such care, contact your local March of Dimes office. They may be able to
help you locate the community resources you need.

The important point is that when you are pregnant, no
matter how old you are, you see your doctor early and
regularly for care.

Staying in School

A generation or two ago, pregnant teens were not al-
lowed to attend school. What a strange system it was to
push a person out of school *because* she was to become a
parent. It's even more important that you continue your
education if you'll be caring for and teaching your child.

You're also likely to need job skills to support your child
whether or not you're with your baby's father. Even if
you're together, or if he provides child support, you're still
likely to work. Chances are you'll want to earn money to

help pay for all the things your child will need. Continuing your education, planning for your career, and learning job skills are especially crucial if you're going to have a baby.

I would have liked to stay home while I was preg-nant, but I had come this far, and I was determined to graduate with my class. I got to enjoy the excitement of graduation like everybody else.

Those who drop out because of pregnancy miss out. A lot of girls look down on themselves when they're pregnant. They think, "I have a baby so I can't graduate." They can do it if they really want to.

You don't have to have a negative attitude about it. The highlight of the senior year is being able to look at your friends and say, "Gosh, we did it. We did it together." You can still do that if you're pregnant.

Elysha

Is there a special school program in your area for preg-nant and parenting teens? Public high schools and some private schools can no longer legally push students out of regular classes because of pregnancy or marital status.

However, if there is a special program, you'd probably take prenatal health and parenting classes there. You'd also be more likely to get help in solving any problems you may have because of your pregnancy. Many pregnant teens have talked to us about the benefits of being with other teens with experiences similar to theirs.

When I first started showing, I was afraid to go out in public because I was ashamed of myself. I didn't want anything to do with being pregnant, but it was a fact of life.

My counselor told me about the Teen Mother Program and suggested I transfer. When I went to TMP, I felt better. I had no idea there were that many

*teens who were pregnant. Until I went there, I thought
I was the only one.*

Liz, pregnant at 15

Even if you haven't started high school yet, hang in
there. You can still work toward high school graduation
while you're pregnant and after you have your baby. Both
you and your baby will be glad you did.

Pregnancy is *not* a disease. One of the most important
things you can do for yourself and your child is to *stay in
school*. Remember, if you're attending public school, you
have a right to be there throughout your pregnancy. You
can return as soon after delivery as you feel able.

If you're in a private school, you may want to check
with your counselor or your principal. If you find you want
or need to leave that school, be sure you transfer to either a
special program for pregnant teens or your local public
school. To repeat, *don't drop out of school!*

Your Parents' Reaction

Some teens find it extremely difficult to tell their parents
about their pregnancy. Perhaps their parents have told their
daughter she would have to leave home if she got pregnant
too soon, or said to their son that he must move out if he
caused a pregnancy.

Parents of pregnant teens react in many different ways.
Most are shocked, many are unhappy, and some blame
themselves for "allowing" this to happen. In fact, many
parents of pregnant teens experience real grief about a
pregnancy which, they feel, will take away their daughter's
or their son's childhood. After a short time, most parents
tend to be supportive of their teens' needs.

*At first my dad cried. He said I was too young, and
that I should think about abortion. I told him I
couldn't do that because I would always wonder.*

My mom seemed sort of happy. She was going to be a grandmother.

Carla, pregnant at 16

Some parents take a long time to get over their shock, as was the case with Christina's family:

When the nurse told me I was pregnant, I went over to my sister's house. She called my aunt, and my aunt told my mom I was pregnant. My mom got furious. All my sisters were mad at me already.

My mom called me at my sister's, and she started screaming at me. "Why did you do that?" She had trusted me. I knew I was wrong in getting pregnant, but I couldn't tell her anything because she was already so mad at me. Everybody was angry, and nobody talked to me.

I moved in with my sister, and she took me to the clinic when I was three or four months along. I stayed with her for four months. I only saw my parents once or twice during that time. They didn't really want to see me then, but I came back home in June. It's working pretty well.

Christina, pregnant at 15

Coming from a culture different from that of most of your friends can make things harder. If your parents grew up with quite different customs than those in your neighborhood, they may find it even more difficult to accept your pregnancy. Lei was 11 when she moved to the United States with her family. She explained:

In my country you don't even get a boyfriend until you're in college and you're at least 20. They think you're a little kid until you're 25. My brother was 17 when he had his first girlfriend, and my parents thought it was too early.

*I got tired of them because they didn't give me a
chance to grow up. They said I couldn't go out with
guys until I was 21. I couldn't even go out with a guy
who was just a friend.*

*I left when I was 16 and moved in with my boy-
friend. Then I got pregnant. They said I could come
home if I'd get an abortion. They said they would
forgive me, and that we would talk about it. I knew
the same thing was going to happen, that they
wouldn't let me see my boyfriend. It was a battle.
They say they hear what I say, but they don't really
think about it.*

*They called me a lot at my boyfriend's house, and
it was real hard. Later my aunt talked to my mom and
said, "She's your only daughter and you have to help
her." So my mother asked us to move back.*

*We didn't really want to, but we did because we
needed to save money for the baby. We got married,
and we moved back. My dad still doesn't accept us
very well.*

Lei, pregnant at 16

If cultural differences are making it extra hard for you
and your parents, try to talk with them. Try to understand
their point of view, and attempt to work out a plan that will
work for all of you.

Effect on Mother/Daughter Relationship

Sometimes a pregnant teen reports that she feels closer
to her mother than she did before. Perhaps the crisis of the
pregnancy helped both mother and daughter forget some of
their past differences. Perhaps her mother feels needed
again by her daughter. Or for some, it's simply the excitement of the coming grandchild. Miranda was only 13 when
she conceived. She commented:

My mom was disappointed when she found out I was pregnant. The pregnancy changed our relationship. I didn't used to tell her things. I didn't talk to her much because I didn't care. Now I tell her stuff, how I feel, what I'm doing. We've gotten closer.

Miranda, pregnant at 13

Coping with their teenage daughter's pregnancy is hard for many parents. If this is the case in your family, try to understand your family's feelings. If you share some of the things you're feeling, they may be a little more understanding.

Perhaps family counseling would help. If you attend church or synagogue, ask your pastor, priest, or rabbi for suggestions as to where to find counseling. Or you could call Family Services for help. Many hospitals and some schools also have support groups for parents.

Is Marriage the Answer?

If you're still with your baby's father, are you considering marriage? Or perhaps you're already married. Thirty years ago, marriage was considered the answer to too-early pregnancy. If the young man didn't want to marry the young woman he'd gotten pregnant, her father was likely to demand that he do so.

Sometimes the couple moved on to many years of happiness together. For many other couples, it didn't work. Teenagers change rapidly as they develop. The interests they had at 16 may be far removed from the interests they will have at 22.

The couple married at 16 may find themselves to be two very different people by the time they're 20. In fact, if the partners in a marriage aren't yet 18, their marriage is four times as likely to fail within a few years as is a marriage between people in their 20s.

If you're with the father of your baby and you choose to be married, or you move in with him, you both might like to read *Teenage Marriage: Coping with Reality* (1988: Morning Glory Press). It's a practical guide written especially for teenage couples. It includes lots of tips on developing a good relationship.

> *When I got pregnant, it was exciting, but scary too. I was very much still my mama's baby. I told my boyfriend who had joined the Army a couple of weeks earlier.*
>
> *He seemed to be fine. I had thought he would be upset. He kept telling me he wanted to get married. I wanted to be sure he wasn't marrying me just because I was pregnant.*
>
> *We didn't see each other until that Christmas when I was already showing, and he was excited. We got married while he was home. We haven't really lived together yet.*
>
> Dawn Ellen, pregnant at 17

> *We got a little apartment, and that was hard. He was working construction. We had only one room in that first apartment, but it was nice.*
>
> *I was still kind of scared because I was away from home. You see, I was always close to my mom. It was exciting, but it was also scary to be out on my own. After we had Francene it was nice, but being a mother is hard.*
>
> Joanne, pregnant at 18

If He's Not With You

Sometimes one's partner seems to change when he learns she's pregnant:

> *We found out I was pregnant when I was three months. It was weird. I didn't know if I should be*

happy or sad. I kind of laughed and cried at the same time. I'm with the father sort of, but he's changed a lot.

Anessa, pregnant at 17

If you aren't with your baby's father, you still have decisions to make. Will you put his name on your baby's birth certificate? Will you file for child support? You probably should.

While you might prefer to pretend this man has nothing to do with your baby, it's your baby's needs that you must respect. It really isn't fair to your child not to have the father help support him.

For insight into fathers' feelings, see chapter 12, "Especially for Dad."

Life Goes On

If you aren't happy about this pregnancy and you don't feel you're ready to be a parent, you may want to consider other alternatives. If you decide to continue your pregnancy, you can still consider an adoption plan. For more information on this very difficult choice, see Chapter 6, "For Some, Adoption Is an Option."

Whether you plan to parent your child yourself or are considering adoption, how you take care of yourself during these coming months matters a great deal. It's up to you to help your baby develop into a healthy newborn.

Some babies are born too small and too soon. If you eat the right foods, don't smoke, drink, or take drugs, and get good prenatal health care, your chances of producing a normal healthy baby are extremely good.

What are you doing for your baby today?

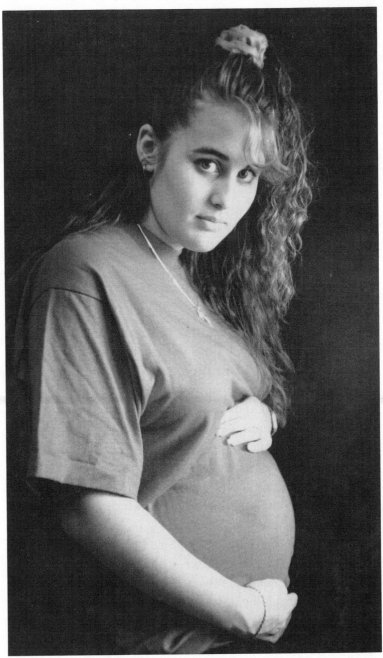

Pregnancy brings changes to one's body.

CHAPTER 2

DEALING WITH MINOR DISCOMFORTS

Newly pregnant young women often comment that they're not used to feeling uncomfortable so often. Pregnancy brings changes in one's body, changes that are sometimes pleasant, sometimes unpleasant. One thing certain—there will be changes.

> *I get real bad back pains, and I had a bladder infection and a bloody nose. It feels weird going through these changes because I was used to being so healthy. And gaining all this weight . . .*
>
> Deborah, pregnant at 17

You can do something about some of these discomforts. First, remember that no one has ever been permanently pregnant—all these things will pass. In fact, some of them will change during your pregnancy.

*My first couple of months up to my fifth I had
morning sickness. My sixth and seventh months were
great.*

                                    LaTisha, pregnant at 15

"I Was Always Tired"

You may feel very tired during your first trimester (the
first three months of your pregnancy). You might be so
tired that you think you're sick and need to stay in bed.
Actually, this tiredness is nature's way of helping your
body shift gears and prepare for the development of your
baby. The hormones shift, and your blood supply changes
places slightly.

*At first I was always tired, and I was sleeping all
day. I didn't know I was pregnant, and Chris kept
saying, "You're pregnant, you're pregnant." Finally I
admitted it.*

                                    Erin, pregnant at 15

Things you can do:

• Take naps.

• Change your position often.

• Figure out activities for which you must be alert. Do
these things early in the day or right after you've
had a nap.

• Exercise even when you feel tired. It really helps.
Taking a walk after lunch or dinner may refresh you
as much as a nap.

Morning Sickness—All Day

Nausea is probably the second most common discomfort
of pregnancy. Many pregnant women feel sick first thing in

the morning, so it's often called morning sickness. It can happen at any time of day, however. In fact, when I (Jean B.) was pregnant, I was most likely to be sick just before dinner. Since I did the cooking, this was especially hard.

> *I was sick all day long for the first four months. I had morning sickness, but I'd throw up all day. I was so weak I couldn't get out of bed. I couldn't even keep my vitamins down. Steve was trying to shove food down me because "You have to take care of the baby," but I was so sick.*
>
> Bethann, pregnant at 17

> *I had morning sickness for three months. It was yukky. I couldn't stand up without feeling like I'd puke or pass out. I lost nearly 15 pounds. The doctor told me to eat crackers and water. I'd go to school, but I'd leave before lunch because the smell of the food would do me in.*
>
> Kellie, pregnant at 16

Things you can do:

- If you feel nauseous, try drinking lukewarm water or tea (decaffeinated) and eating soda crackers.

- Eating small meals more often may help. Don't worry too much about weight gain at this point. Concentrate on feeling better and eating from as many foods groups as you can manage.

- Be sure to check with your doctor before you use over-the-counter medications to relieve nausea. Some of these medicines could harm your baby, but others are just fine.

- If you feel your vitamins are causing nausea, try taking them at different times of the day.

"Where's the Bathroom?"

As your uterus enlarges and your hormones shift, you'll probably have to urinate more often than usual. This is normal early in pregnancy, and will be troublesome again during the last two or three months before your baby is born.

> **If any of these things happen,** *call your doctor*:
> - You have a burning sensation when you urinate
> - You feel you have to urinate, but little comes out
> - Urinating is painful

These symptoms may indicate a bladder infection. Drinking liquids often helps with this condition. If you're nauseous, however, this may be difficult.

> *I knew I was pregnant by two months. I was fine except for four or five bladder infections. One time I had it so bad I thought I was in labor. I'd go to the doctor and get medication each time.*
>
> Marsha, pregnant at 15

If you feel dizzy, try this position.

Are You Dizzy?

Your blood supply changes as your rapidly growing uterus draws new circulation to the lower abdomen. As a result, you may sometimes feel dizzy, especially after you stand for a long time.

If this happens, lie down with your feet higher than your head. If you can't do that, sit down and put your head between your knees. Breathe as deeply as possible. If you feel dizzy toward the end of pregnancy, you'll probably have to lie down.

Moodiness Strikes Again

Do your moods change for no apparent reason? Do you find you're often crabby with your boyfriend or your little brother? I (Jeanne L.) remember suddenly breaking into tears at strange times when I was pregnant. Sometimes I couldn't figure out why I was crying.

Think back to when you first began having periods. You may have had similar feelings because the hormones in your body were changing. Now those hormones are acting up even more as your body prepares for your coming baby. This in itself causes moodiness in many pregnant women.

> *I was scared and I was embarrassed. I'd seen my sisters pregnant, and I knew how they looked. I didn't want to look like that. I had never been fat in my life, and when I got pregnant, I hated it. I wondered, "Why do I have to gain so much weight? Why does my body have to change?"*
>
> Meghan, pregnant at 17

You may have lots of things on your mind—so many decisions to make, so much to do. The reactions of your parents, your friends, or your baby's father may not be what you'd like. You might call it mental overload.

*I was always embarrassed when I'd walk by guys I
knew. Are they thinking, "Oh, she's pregnant and
he's not there"? I was getting sick every morning and
nobody knew. When the girls at school hear you're
pregnant and you aren't with the father, they make all
kinds of accusations.*

Meghan

Sometimes a pregnant woman may not be interested in
things that were important to her only a few weeks ago. If
this happens to you, your family and friends will probably
be confused. They may give you advice, too much advice.
When you begin to feel your baby move at about 16 weeks,
however, you may experience a new focus on life.

You May Have Heartburn

Your last trimester will bring some different complaints,
complaints mostly related to your body's larger size.

*It's not fun being pregnant. You've got all these
responsibilities. And the weight! I gained maybe two
pounds a month for five or six months, then suddenly I
practically blew up. I'm up to 152, and my normal
weight is 120.*

LaTisha, 15, nine months pregnant

Your uterus is now so big that you can feel pressure in
your stomach area. Heartburn is a common complaint.

Things you can do:

• Eat frequent small meals.

• Avoid greasy foods.

• Add more fruits and vegetables to your diet.

Many moms have problems with constipation during the
last six weeks or so of pregnancy. These same tactics will
also help you avoid this discomfort.

Backaches

The weight you carry now on the front side of your body is pulling against your back. As your spine adapts to this extra weight, you may have backaches.

If you exercise throughout your pregnancy, you're less likely to have pain in your back. Hopefully, you haven't waited until your last trimester to do so. The exercises you learn in your childbirth preparation class will also help.

Things you can do:
- Heat may make your back feel better. You can use a heating pad. Some doctors recommend that you don't go in a hot tub (jacuzzi) during pregnancy. Check with your doctor.

- Massage feels good too, so accept any offers for a backrub.

- Resting with your legs elevated helps both your back and your legs.

- Squat down to pick things up from the floor. Avoid bending foreward from your waist.

- Remember to stand with your knees relaxed. This keeps your back and leg muscles relaxed too.

If You Can't Sleep

*By eight months, I started getting tired again, and now I'm **really** tired. I can't get comfortable. I can't sleep.*

LaTisha

Insomnia, or sleeplessness, is a frequent discomfort in the last few months of pregnancy. There are several reasons and several solutions. Your uterus, now much larger, is

Pillows can help you sleep better.

pressing against several organs. One result is shortness of breath. Another is back problems.

The illustration above shows you how you can position several pillows under your body to help you feel better. Try it. This is such a relaxing position that you may sleep this way for awhile after delivery too.

Pregnancy Isn't Permanent

Most moms begin to feel permanently pregnant about this time. As we mentioned before, nobody has ever been pregnant forever. That fact doesn't help much, however, when you *feel* that way.

> *During pregnancy I had excruciating pain in my tailbone. It could have been the pressure. The last month was horrible because I was so big I could hardly walk. I'd go to the mall, then actually could not walk because I'd get sharp pains. I got sweaty a lot because I'd be so hot. I'd find my stomach hitting the breadboard in the kitchen because it stuck out so far.*
>
> Courtney, pregnant at 15

Rest when you can, use makeup, take the time to dress carefully. If you can afford it, buy a new maternity outfit in your favorite color for those last weeks.

Many expectant moms (and dads too) have dreams about their unborn babies. It's a happy and normal experience. It is not, however, a guarantee as to how your baby will look or what gender s/he will be. Enjoy them for what they are—dreams.

You may or may not be involved with anyone sexually during your pregnancy. Those who are may have questions about what is okay at this time. Sexual activity is fine with one or two exceptions. Bleeding, pain, or a rupture of the membranes (broken water bag) are reasons to avoid sexual intercourse. Other sexual activities are all right. In fact, many couples experience exceptional closeness during pregnancy. Recommendations for after delivery are discussed in Chapter 9.

You probably will have a fairly comfortable pregnancy if you follow the suggestions in this chapter. And most important, you can look forward to a new you as your baby's mother.

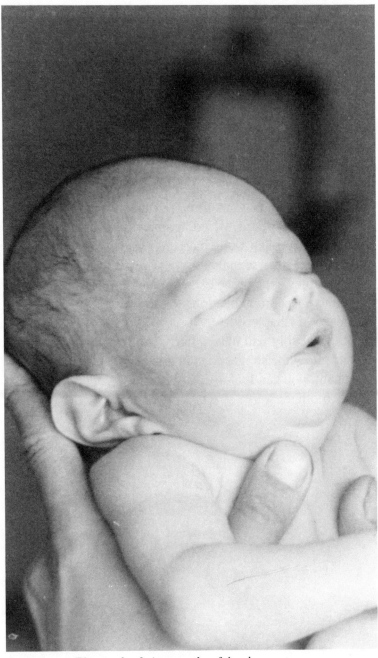

The result of nine months of development . . .

CHAPTER 3

YOUR BABY'S DEVELOPMENT

Each of us has something in common with the baby growing within you. That wonderful thing is that we all began the same way. Our father's sperm united with our mother's ovum and here we are!

Getting here involved a mysterious journey. That first union took place in our mother's fallopian tube. At that point, we looked like a ball of cells. That ball of cells grew rapidly as it moved down the four-inch long tube into the uterus, then spent a day or two deciding just where to implant itself. Your baby was developing like this before you missed your first period. During this time, the number of cells increases rapidly. This process is called *proliferation.*

Proliferation: Making a lot of something,
usually quickly.

Female and Male Reproductive Organs

The following diagrams of female and male genitals are intended to help you better understand your body and your partner's body. Learning the correct names of the parts of your body will make it easier to talk with your doctor and your partner.

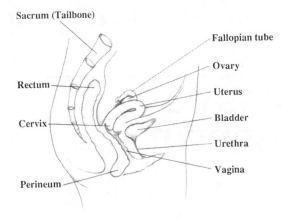

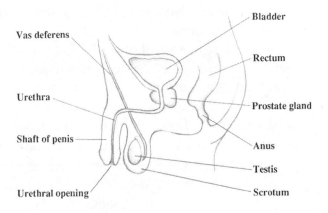

Cells Continue to Divide

By the time your period is two weeks late and you're getting that pregnancy test, the cells within you have begun a process called *differentiation*. Up to now the cells have looked pretty much alike. Now they're beginning to sort themselves out.

Differentiation: Sorting things out, putting things together that are alike.

Characteristics called "chromosomes" will guide each cell's growth.

Chromosomes: The basic cell part containing inherited things.

Both mother and father have 23 pairs of these chromosomes. Each parent gives one from each pair to their baby. Eye and hair color are decided this way. The baby's gender is determined by which chromosome the father gives to the baby.

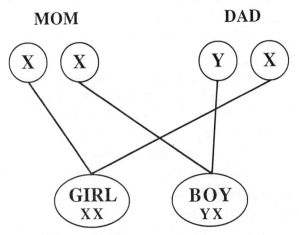

Dad's chromosome "chooses" boy or girl.

By the end of your first month of
pregnancy, your baby is 1/2 inch long.
Your baby's arms, legs and shoulders
have barely begun to appear. The eyes
are present though we don't think baby
sees yet. Baby's brain cells are already
developing.

*Four weeks
drawn to
actual size.*

Second and Third Months (5 - 13 1/2 weeks)

During the next month, your
baby doubles in length and the
organs of the abdomen begin to
develop. At eight weeks the baby
is called a fetus. Before that time,
s/he was called an embryo.

There isn't really a skeleton yet
as the arms and legs are barely
beginning. The body is mainly
working on the development of
internal organs such as the liver,
stomach, gall bladder and spleen.
Tiny fingers are beginning to

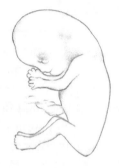

*Eleven weeks
drawn to actual size.*

develop. The baby's tongue and teeth can also be found.
The heart pumps blood.

During the third month she will grow to about 31/2 to 4
inches in length. Her brain is making very rapid growth at
this time. By the end of this month all the parts of her body
will be started. The rest of pregnancy will be devoted to
fine tuning them—helping them grow bigger and more
efficient and able to operate on their own without your
blood supply for nourishment.

During this period your baby's sexual organs develop.
Now we could tell whether you're going to have a boy or
girl baby.

By the tenth week your baby's fingerprints are identifiable for life. Years ago criminals tried having their fingerprints changed by plastic surgeons so they wouldn't get caught. They learned, however, that the change only lasted about a month. After that, the new skin changed back into the original fingerprint.

The criminal, just like you, me, and your baby, had his permanent fingerprint when he was about ten weeks gestation. Pretty amazing!

Fourth Month Ends (18 weeks)

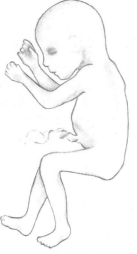

By the end of the fourth month, baby is four to five inches long, roughly the size of the flat part of his daddy's hand. The muscles and skin of baby's face now reflect an inherited pattern—you could tell who he looks like!

Tiny fingernails begin to grow. His lungs, the last organ to mature, begin to breathe amniotic fluid.

As your body enlarges, you may notice that some days you feel bigger than others. This is partly because the amount of fluid around the baby varies as he breathes and drinks the fluid. You will continue to notice this variation throughout pregnancy.

*Sixteen weeks
drawn to actual size.*

Incidentally, when your doctor talks about how far along in your pregnancy you are, s/he usually refers to the number of weeks or months LMP. This means the amount of time since your last menstrual period. When you talk about the number of months you are pregnant, you're probably talking about the time since you conceived. If your timing doesn't match your doctor's, this might be the reason.

Checking on Your Baby

Your doctor may discuss a procedure called an *ultrasound*. This is done in a doctor's office or at a laboratory.

Ultrasound: An examination using sonar
or radio-like waves to trace the outline
of the baby in the uterus.

An ultrasound, which doesn't hurt at all, is done mainly to see how far the baby's growth has progressed and to confirm the due date. It can also determine the presence of certain birth defects and sometimes the gender of the baby. If you have an ultrasound, you may receive a copy of the picture of the baby—although it won't look like a photograph.

Several times during your pregnancy the doctor will have blood tests done. One will show your blood type. Another is called AFP (alpha feta protein), and it measures the protein in your blood. Many doctors do this test instead of the ultrasound.

Another test sometimes done at about 16 weeks gestation is called *amniocentesis*. In this test, fluid from the uterus is removed with a long needle and sent to a special laboratory.

This fluid can be tested to reveal the baby's gender, and many other characteristics including such rare genetic conditions as Down syndrome. This test doesn't hurt much. It's like any injection with a needle.

About 75 percent of pregnant women are given an ultrasound, but only five to ten percent take the amniocentesis test. If you have an amniocentesis, you won't know the results for about two weeks, and they're reported like a blood test. If this is done, you can get a picture of your baby's chromosomes.

You'll Feel Him Move

By the twentieth week, halfway through pregnancy, your baby will weigh almost 1 1/2 pounds and be about 12 inches long. Since the baby opens and closes her eyes, we know she is experiencing a variety of things. She senses light and dark. She may suck her thumb at times. Now you can feel her moving around inside of you.

The doctor can easily hear your baby's heart beating now, and will check that every time you go in for a visit. Baby's ears are also developed by this time, and she sometimes moves in response to loud sounds.

A few years ago, researchers tried to learn what the baby hears at this stage. One woman they interviewed was a cello player. During her pregnancy she was preparing for a musical performance. She played a favorite song every day during her pregnancy. The cello rested against her body where the baby was most likely to hear it. She discovered that after her baby was born, she could calm him by playing that same song. It didn't matter to her baby whether she actually played the piece on her cello or used a recording.

Sixth Month—Not Ready to Be Born

By the 24th week your baby should weigh about 1 1/2 pounds. If he is born now, he has less than a fifty-fifty chance to live. If he does survive, he is likely to have lifelong disabilities.

Your baby now has hair, eyelashes, and that fine baby hair you may have noticed on newborn babies. It is called *lanugo*. The baby also is covered with a creamy substance called *vernix*. This is a cream that nature provides to make his skin soft. When your baby is born you may notice it, especially in the folds of his skin.

Baby can now cry, but very weakly. If born at this time, his lungs probably wouldn't be ready to work well.

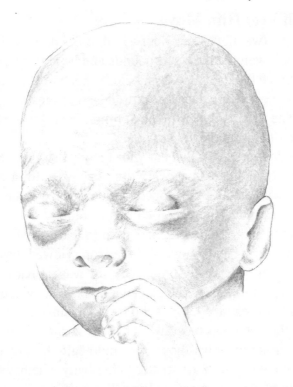

At 24 weeks your baby is fully formed—but not yet ready
for life on the outside.

Baby Feels Crowded

When I was about eight months pregnant, I got
scared because I couldn't feel him move. He'd been
moving a lot, so I went to the hospital. They told me
he wasn't moving because he was so big. They said he
didn't have room to move!

Estela, pregnant at 17

During the last ten weeks of pregnancy, the baby gains
weight by making fat. She has had very little fat up to now.
Most of us don't especially like the idea of adding fat, but it
is an important part of the body. It is a reserve of energy for
rapid growth which will continue even after the baby is

born. It also insulates your baby from heat and cold.

Fat gives the body softness and curves which cushion impact and make the pleasant cuddly feeling we associate with babies. While theoretically your baby can live outside the uterus at this time, most

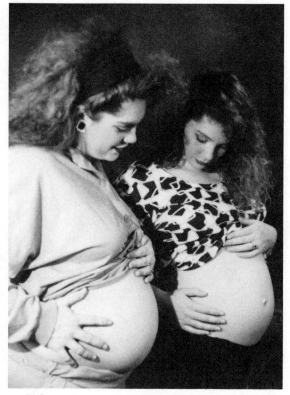

Baby and you gain rapidly in the last months.

babies who are born before 36 weeks gestation spend ten to twelve weeks in the hospital "finishing" their development. They often suffer complications of their immaturity which may or may not be outgrown.

At 40 weeks, the average baby weighs 7 1/2 pounds and is 20-22 inches long. His mother will have gained at least 25 pounds during her pregnancy. The rest of the weight she gained is for her body's use.

Your baby's journey from conception to delivery is a wonderful and fascinating journey. The next two chapters tell you how you can help make that journey a healthy one for your child. *It's up to you.*

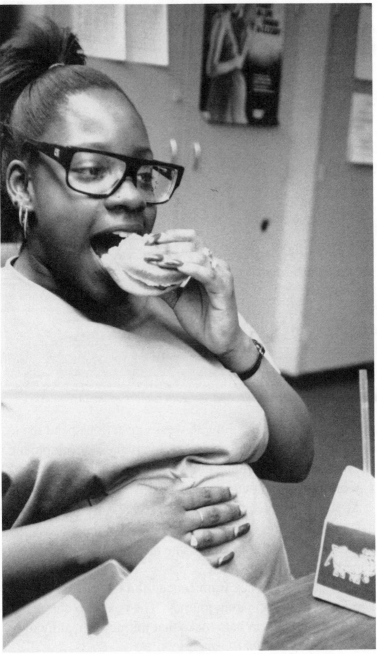

When you eat healthy foods, both you and baby feel better.

CHAPTER 4

EATING RIGHT FOR BABY AND YOU

My boyfriend eats vegetables, and I find myself craving vegetables. I drink a lot of milk. I don't really like it, but I drink it because I know the baby needs it. I take my vitamins all the time, and even though I don't like meat too much, I make sure I have enough. I want the healthiest baby possible.

Anessa, pregnant at 17

"If she doesn't start eating better, I'm getting out of here before I'm supposed to," says the fetus in "Inside My Mom," a video produced by the March of Dimes Birth Defects Foundation. The hero of the film is a cartoon fetus who is concerned about his mother's diet. His point is that babies of poorly nourished mothers are likely to be born too early.

The little fetus continues to talk about his mother's eating habits. "Oh good! She's finally getting me something to eat," he exclaims.

In the next scene, his mother is buying from a junk food machine. The little fetus moans, "Oh no! Just a candy bar. Doesn't she know I need *real* food?"

Before long, however, his mother's doctor convinces her that she should eat healthy foods so she will have a healthy baby. She starts eating foods from the Basic Four food groups, and the little fetus is delighted.

> *You need to take care of yourself and eat right. My sister's baby was barely five pounds when he was born, and I think it was because she didn't eat right. All I'd see her do was drink soda and eat chips and candy. We'd tell her to eat, and she'd say, "No, I don't want it."*
>
> Alice Ann, 15 - Vincent, 3 weeks

Remember, if you're under 18 and pregnant, you need all the good foods an older pregnant woman needs *plus* two extra glasses of milk. You need that extra milk because your bones are still growing.

> *I didn't know you should drink all that milk. When I learned more about nutrition, I started to eat good. Nutrition is really important to the baby. It's best if you can start eating right early in your pregnancy.*
>
> Beth, 18 - Patty, 3 weeks

You also need to drink some water each day. Water is much better than soda for you and for your baby.

Your Baby Eats What You Eat

You know now how your baby is developing inside you. Your next step is to learn what you can do to help your baby grow. Is your goal to make a good baby without gaining too much weight? You want a healthy baby, and you probably don't want to be fat after you deliver.

Good nutrition throughout pregnancy is essential if both mother and baby are to develop well.

Okay, so what do you need to eat when you're pregnant? There is no magic formula other than what you've already heard about nutrition in your health classes. Only now it's your baby who will suffer if you eat only junk food.

You need food from the Basic Four food groups every day:

Meat, poultry, fish, eggs, and beans: 2-3 servings

Dairy products—milk, yogurt, cheese: 4-6 servings

Grains—bread, cereal, noodles, spaghetti: 6 servings

Fruits and vegetables: 6 servings

You needed these foods before you were pregnant, but now you need even more of some of them. If you're nauseated, have heartburn, or changes in your appetite, eating will be a special problem for you.

I couldn't worry about nutrition the first four or five months because I was so sick. Later on I ate good because I wanted a healthy baby. I loved him already, and I knew if I ate bad, he could be all little and that scared me. Little babies scare me, but he came out about 8 pounds.

Kellie, 15 - Kevin, 3 months

Do you ever have heartburn? Fats, spicy foods, coffee, chocolate, spearmint and peppermint all may contribute to heartburn. So do alcohol and nicotine.

If you aren't eating any of these foods, drinking, or smoking, and you still have heartburn, try smaller meals, but eat more often.

A midnight snack may help prevent morning sickness. It also may help solve sleeping problems at the end of pregnancy.

Your family may like to eat fast foods often, or they may have other eating habits that don't fit into the best pregnancy diet. If so, you need to consider your reality, what's possible and available for you to eat. Then you work from there to get the foods so important to both you and your baby.

Good Nutrition Helps Prevent Eclampsia

Another important issue in pregnancy is eclampsia (toxemia). Eclampsia is a condition some mothers develop during the last few weeks of pregnancy.

Signs and Symptoms of Eclampsia

- **Extremely high blood pressure** (That's why they always take your blood pressure at the doctor's.)
- **Severe and persistent headaches**
- **Blurry vision**
- **Sudden, rapid weight gain with severe swelling in the legs**
- **Eventually, convulsions**

Some swelling is normal because your body is storing liquid for its future needs. However, a sudden, rapid weight gain with severe swelling in your legs, ankles, and fingers could be a symptom of eclampsia.

Some people feel eating too much salt causes this swelling. If your doctor notices any symptoms of eclampsia, s/he may ask you to cut out most of the salt in your diet. If this happens, you need to cooperate. Generally, however, if you're eating a well balanced diet, you can eat a reasonable amount of salt without worrying.

Eclampsia can be a serious problem. It's the main cause of childbirth-related deaths of mothers in the developed nations of the world.

We're not trying to frighten you. We're also not suggesting that if you eat poorly once in a while you're going to die. The message, however, is that we're not talking simply about a beauty issue as we discuss nutrition in pregnancy.

Two things are known to help prevent eclampsia. One is regular prenatal care. *See your doctor regularly.* The other is eating enough protein.

Importance of Protein

Babies whose mothers eat plenty of protein have more brain cells than do babies whose mothers eat less than three servings of protein foods each day during pregnancy. More brain cells mean a smarter baby!

Protein foods include all kinds of meat, fish, and poultry. Peanut butter, refried beans with cheese, baked beans, and eggs are also high in protein. So is the milk you drink. Cereal, bread, pasta, and a few other foods also contain some protein.

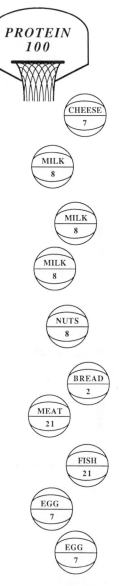

Think of each basketball as a serving of protein. Put them all together and you have a day's supply of protein.

BABY NEEDS: 5 Servings
MILK OR CHOCOLATE MILK
☐☐☐ *or trade any 1 glass for* ☐☐
1 slice American cheese *or* 6 oz. yogurt
or 1" cube any cheese *or* 1/2 cup ice cream
or 1/2 cup cottage cheese

The cow suggests possible substitutes for milk.

Milk for Baby's Bones, Teeth

It's hard to think of a pregnant mom's diet without thinking about milk. Besides being a good source of the much needed protein, milk provides calcium. Your growing baby needs a lot of calcium for building bones and teeth.

If you like milk, drink four to six glasses each day. If you don't drink milk, get your calcium from other foods. See the cow above for some foods which supply the same amount of protein and calcium as one large glass of milk.

It's okay to add chocolate to your milk—but remember you're adding calories, too.

Adding fruit to six ounces of plain yogurt gives you even more protein than six ounces of premixed yogurt. You can add fruit, fresh or canned, as you eat it. Mixing the fruit in yourself also saves you money. Do other family members tend to eat up your yogurt? Perhaps they'll be more likely to leave the plain yogurt for you and your baby.

Melting a slice of cheese on a piece of bread for breakfast or lunch adds the protein of bread to your meal along with the calcium and protein in the cheese.

Fruits and Vegetables

Fruits and vegetables contain water and carbohydrates which give you lots of energy. Most important, they are good sources of vitamins and minerals. Generally, the darker the color, the richer the food is in vitamins and minerals. For instance, broccoli and spinach are richer in vitamins than plain lettuce or celery.

Eating a variety of fruits and vegetables will give you a good balance in your diet. Fruits and vegetables are at least as good for you raw as they are cooked. If you eat tomato and lettuce with your hamburger, you're getting a serving of vegetables.

If you don't like vegetables, you can get most of these nutrients in fruit. Fruit on your cereal counts as one of the six servings you need daily.

Eating plenty of fruits and vegetables also helps prevent constipation.

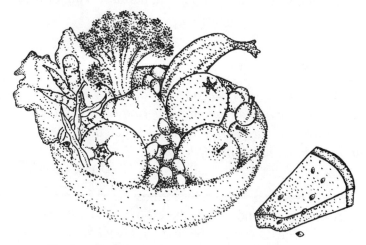

You have lots of choices for your fruits and vegetables.

Cereals and Bread

Almost everyone likes the foods in this group. They include all the cereals and all the breads as well as

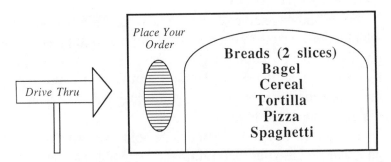

You can get your breads and cereals while you're out.

spaghetti, macaroni, rice, corn, oats, tortillas, and pizza crust. Choose sugar-free cereals because of the lower calorie and higher fiber content. The fiber helps prevent constipation, a common complaint during pregnancy.

Another plus for this group is that they contain some protein. If you eat the six servings you need daily, you'll have as much protein as you'd get in half a serving of meat or fish.

Take Your Vitamins

I was really sick. I was anemic, and they were always taking blood from me. The first few months I didn't want to eat at all. I always gagged and threw up my first month to my fifth month.

Elisa Marie, 15 - Delila, 9 months

Anemia: A condition of the blood which causes tiredness, a "dull" feeling, and weakness.

Few of us eat a perfect diet every day. For that reason, and because you and your baby need lots of vitamins and minerals, your doctor will recommend that you take prenatal vitamins.

Sometimes moms complain that the vitamins leave an aftertaste. If that's a problem for you, try taking your vitamin after a larger meal, whether that's lunch or dinner. You'll digest your vitamin more slowly with your meal which may cut out the aftertaste.

You may already have regular vitamins at home, or you may see a brand that's cheaper than those prescribed by your doctor. Is it okay to take those instead? Not really. Prenatal vitamins contain extra amounts of vitamins and minerals you especially need during pregnancy. Most important are folic acid and iron.

Pregnant women need more iron because they're making additional blood for themselves and their baby. Recent research also showed that pregnant teens who take enough iron every day have a far better attention span than pregnant students who are careless about getting enough.

So, stick to those prenatal vitamins all during your pregnancy. In fact, some doctors recommend that moms

More milk for baby and you.

continue taking them for a few weeks after delivery because they help them feel better.

If there's another child around, be sure to keep your prenatal vitamins out of reach. The high iron levels in prenatal vitamins can make a young child quite sick.

Limit the Fat

What about fat and calories? How a food is prepared is as important as what it contains before it's cooked. For instance, you add about 90 calories when you fry eggs in a tablespoon of butter. Fried eggs are fine if they're prepared in a teflon-coated pan without added fat. Adding a teaspoon or so of water will keep them from sticking, yet won't change the taste at all.

Other foods high in fat include lunch meat, hot dogs, sweet breads, desserts such as pie or cream puffs, and, of course, anything deep fried.

Calories Count

When I got pregnant, it was exciting. I think I ate everything in sight. I did a lot of walking, but I gained a lot of weight anyhow. That's why I'm so heavy now.
                                                        LuAnn, 20 - Eddie, 4

When you're low on energy, it's tempting to have a candy bar or doughnut. Within an hour, however, that energy surge is gone and you're feeling listless again. Snacks such as fresh fruit, peanuts, yogurt, or milk will give you energy that lasts longer. As a bonus, these foods give baby more energy too.

Calories do count during pregnancy. A pregnant teen-ager should be able to eat 2500 to 3000 calories per day. If you stay within this limit and you're getting a reasonable amount of exercise, you'll probably gain between 28 and 40 pounds, the amount recommended by most doctors.

  If you're 17 or younger and still growing, you may need to gain more weight. It's important that you show a slow steady gain from about your eighth week until your baby is born.

  So often pregnant teenagers think that if they gain much weight, they'll not be able to get back into their jeans and bikinis. If they were eating a lot of of junk food before pregnancy (as too many non-pregnant teenagers seem to do), they may continue this way of eating. If she has french

Your baby appreciates a healthy snack.

fries and a coke for a snack very often, a pregnant 16-year-old either won't have any appetite for the nutritious foods she needs, or her weight will shoot up far higher than she or her doctor wants. Gaining 50 to 60 pounds during those nine months isn't healthy either.

> *This time I'm not going to overeat. I'm going to watch my weight, eat good, but not gain too much. Last time I went from 115 to 180 pounds. I'm still ten pounds away from my normal weight—and I'm pregnant again!*
>
> Eileen, 18 - Jackie, 17 months

The Fast Food Dilemma

Many people eat fast foods. Some teens appear almost to live on hamburgers, french fries, and soda. Sometimes people say fast foods are junk foods. Some of them, such as sodas, add empty calories to your diet. If you know what's good for you, however, you can continue to enjoy occasional fast foods without feeling guilty.

Let's compare some choices:

	PROTEIN	CALORIES	FAT
Double bacon cheeseburger	42 gm	890	55%
Reg. size fries	8 gm	360	45%
Reg size soda	0	243	0
Total	**50 gm**	**1493**	**50%**

Perhaps this doesn't look so bad. You get half the calories and half the protein you need each day. This meal, however, has some glaring faults:

• It doesn't leave much room for calories for the rest of your day.

• It includes very little vegetable and no fruit.

• It's high in fat—which means more fat on *your* body. Ideally, your meals will contain no more than 30 percent fat.

Now let's compare the hamburger, fries, and soda with chicken, salad, and milk:

	PROTEIN	CALORIES	FAT
Charbroiled chicken (not fried)	28 gm	320	17%
10 oz. low fat milk	13 gm	175	2%
Salad with blue cheese dressing	3 gm	150	75%
Total	**44 gm**	**645**	**30%**

This meal gives you almost as much protein (plenty for one meal) as the hamburger, french fries, and soda. If you eat the chicken, milk, and salad, you'll get only about one quarter of your daily calorie allowance. Even with the salad dressing, it has much less fat. You'll feel full, you'll feel good—and you won't need extra situps to get rid of the calories.

Be careful of foods described as "lite." For instance, one fast food chain's "lite" potato is more than 50 percent fat, contains almost 300 calories, and has only 7 grams of protein. That's *not* a good deal nutritionwise.

Follow the Basic Four

If you don't want to figure out every meal like this, just follow the simple Basic Four food groups theory. Plan to have three meat group servings, five dairy foods, six breads and cereals, and six fruits and vegetables each day. Avoid foods that have lots of fat or are "empty" calories, and you should feel good and have a healthy baby.

Eat the foods you need all through your pregnancy. *Your baby will appreciate you!*

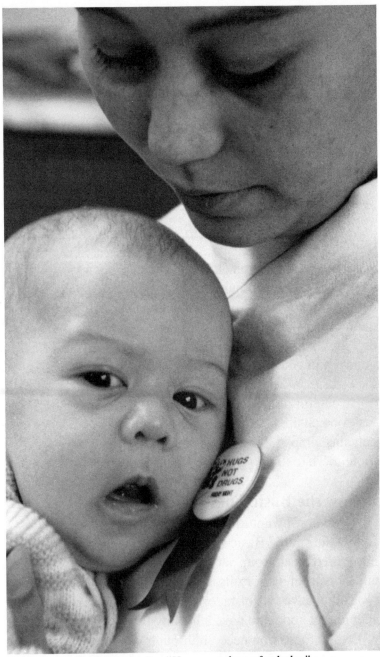

Her pin says it—"Hugs, not drugs for baby."

CHAPTER 5

"NO" TO SMOKING, DRUGS, ALCOHOL

Some people, when they're confused or concerned about something, turn to drugs, alcohol or smoking to comfort themselves. When we consider the danger to the fetus if the mother smokes (including pot), uses drugs, or drinks liquor, however, it's clear that these activities are a form of abusing a child—even though that child is not yet born.

Smoking Harms Fetus

Do you smoke? If you're pregnant, you could do you and your child a big favor by stopping.

I used to smoke a lot. Then one day Tim told me he didn't want to kiss me because I smelled like an ash tray. Then Angel, who was 2, was breaking up my cigarettes and leaving them all over. Tim said "See, Angel wants you to quit."

I said, "Everyone in my family smokes."
He said, "Well, you don't have to."
He wouldn't buy me cigarettes. He said he'd buy me anything else. Finally when I got pregnant with Kenny, Tim and I sat down and I told him, "I think it's going to be real hard for me. My body is telling me I want to smoke and the baby is telling me I shouldn't smoke." And I did have one terrible week. I went a whole week without smoking, and I ate and I ate and I ate.

And then I realized how a smoker smells. I can't stand it.

Then after that one week, I didn't want to smoke—in fact, smoke bothered me. My family would blow smoke in my face because they thought I'd want a cigarette. I'd tell them I didn't want to smoke.

And then I realized how a smoker smells. I can't stand it. My brother smokes, and when he walks in, he smells awful. I'm glad I quit.

Meghan, 25 - Angel, 8; Kenny, 6; Jose, 2; Leon, 8 months

Baby Can't "Breathe"

Each time you smoke, your baby has a hard time "breathing" inside you. A fetus doesn't breathe as we do, of course, but when his mother smokes, he gets less oxygen. Recent research shows that the fetus may even be in distress when his mother is in a smoke-filled room. Being in a room with smokers causes the baby to be more uneasy since he isn't getting enough oxygen.

I smoked a lot the first four months I was pregnant. I was horribly upset. Inside I knew I was pregnant by two months, but I wouldn't admit it, even to myself, for another two months. So I was always nervous and had to have cigarettes.

I'd smoke one or two packs a day trying to convince myself I wasn't pregnant. I was just a basket case, crying and smoking, smoking and crying all the time.

I went to the doctor when I was four months pregnant. When I finally accepted the fact I was pregnant, I cut back on my smoking. Then in my last month I got this real hang-up about smoking—even though I hadn't seen Karl yet. I suddenly wanted to do this for him (or her—I didn't know which yet). So I just quit. Then I couldn't stand someone else smoking—it almost made me sick.

I'm still not smoking. I feel I should do everything I can to influence Karl not to smoke. If I get upset and want to smoke, I get a coke or a glass of water or sometimes a carrot or a toothpick, anything but a cigarette. I know if I smoke even one, I'll start again, so I simply can't have that first one.

Kimberly, 17 - Karl, 23 months

Smokers May Have Smaller Babies

Pregnant women who smoke cigarettes tend to have smaller babies who gain weight slowly. That's because the uterine temperature drops when mom smokes, and the baby must struggle to keep warm. That effort uses lots of energy, energy the baby would otherwise use to gain weight.

These babies also have more colds and pneumonia than other babies. There are more miscarriages, stillbirths, and sudden infant deaths among babies whose mothers smoked.

I wanted to quit smoking when I got pregnant, but I couldn't. I knew all the health risks to myself and to

my baby, but that wasn't helping. Finally I took a
stop-smoking class at school, mostly because I needed
the credit to graduate.

You had to write down every time you wanted a
cigarette, what you were doing at the time, and what
you could do instead of smoking. I decided to see if it
would work. I was already seven months pregnant,
but I managed to quit.

Angelica, 20 - Shaun, 3

We researched the effects of smoking among students in
our school. Thirty-nine babies were born to students in our
special program for pregnant teenagers that year. Four of
the babies weighed less than six pounds. The mothers of
three of those babies smoked during pregnancy. Almost no
one else in the class smoked.

As soon as I found out I was pregnant, I quit
smoking because they say you can have a premature
baby. I didn't want to take any chances. It's only nine
months not to smoke, and you might as well not risk
it. After all, it's another life inside you. I did the same
thing with drinking.

Cheryl, 16 - Racquelle, 2 months

Fetal Alcohol Syndrome (FAS)

I was into pot and alcohol pretty bad. Once after I
was a few weeks pregnant, I got mad at Jim, so I got
drunk, and I was scared. But Orlando's okay, and
now I'm going to stay clear of it all. I don't want to
be afraid next time. I know that drinking or smoking
dope is not going to help matters. It'll make it worse.

Holly, 17 - Orlando, 5 months

If you're pregnant, think before you drink—then *don't!*
Fetal Alcohol Syndrome (FAS) is a condition affecting

babies whose mothers drank alcohol during pregnancy. We know that alcohol can cause a pattern of physical and mental defects in the fetus.

An FAS baby may be abnormally small at birth, especially in head size. Unlike most small newborns, the FAS baby never catches up in growth. Most of these youngsters have smaller than average brains resulting in mild to severe mental retardation. They are often jittery and have behavior problems. Almost half of the FAS babies have heart defects which may require surgery.

---

*"Fetal Alcohol Syndrome (FAS)
is one birth defect
the mother alone can prevent."*

The worst thing for a pregnant woman to do is go on a binge. Lots of drinking at once is especially risky for the fetus. There is no known safe level of alcohol use for pregnant women, particularly during the first three months when the baby's vital organs are developing.

"To be safe, forget about drinking throughout pregnancy," cautions Anita Gallegos, former Director of Community Services, March of Dimes Birth Defects Foundation, Southern California Chapter. "This is one birth defect the mother alone can prevent."

Friends would say, "Oh, just a little (liquor) won't hurt." But I didn't. I was always trying to think back to those first two or three months, wondering if I had done a lot of things that would harm her. I worried that my baby might not be all right. Smoking is bad enough, but drugs and alcohol—I don't see how anybody could do that during pregnancy.

Beth, 18 - Patty, 3 weeks

Drugs and Pregnancy

Taking drugs during pregnancy is endangering your child. Don't take any unless your doctor prescribes them.

Illegal drugs have lifelong effects on babies. A baby exposed to drugs before she is born may be mentally retarded and have learning disabilities, language delays, hyperactivity, poor play skills, and numerous other conditions that interfere with normal life. Babies who are born

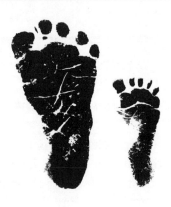

Guess which baby's mother did drugs while she was pregnant.

If you're pregnant, see a doctor now.
Fight low birthweight.
March of Dimes
Campaign For Healthier Babies

addicted also often have permanent physical disabilities. If they are identified at birth as addicted, they may not be permitted to be with their mother. Instead, they could be placed in foster care.

Learning disabilities may not show up until the child goes to school. Many of the effects of cocaine, crack, and crystal (crank) are not noticed at birth, and the parents may think they were lucky. Crack, cocaine, and crystal all have the same effects. All three cause small holes in the brain.

Children prenatally exposed to drugs are likely to have social problems that keep them from making friends easily. How lonely they must be.

Marijuana smoking also affects your unborn baby. Besides reducing the baby's oxygen supply, the results of the drug can cause a boy baby to have a very small penis.

Babies born to mothers who are addicted to heroin are likely to be pathetic little creatures who go through withdrawal after birth. These tiny babies experience the same kind of agony an adult experiences who, after becoming addicted to heroin, goes off it cold turkey.

Most of us know not to take "hard" drugs during pregnancy. But did you know that drugs sold "over the counter" can also be a problem to a fetus? The right dose for mother generally means baby is getting a huge overdose.

Many drugs have been shown to be harmful to the fetus, so many that March of Dimes literature stresses, "Take no drugs, not even a nose spray, aspirin, or Tums, unless your doctor prescribes it." And your doctor will undoubtedly agree with the March of Dimes. Laxatives are especially dangerous during pregnancy.

There is no good time to use drugs, alcohol, or nicotine, but during pregnancy is the worst time. Help your baby to a healthy start.

Don't drink, smoke, or do drugs!

Teen birthmothers tell their stories.

CHAPTER **6**

FOR SOME— ADOPTION IS AN OPTION

You may be thinking, "Me? Make an adoption plan? You're crazy!" In any group of pregnant teens, a few will consider the adoption option. Even fewer will actually carry out the adoption plan. Nevertheless, we're spending a chapter on this subject for several reasons:

- If you're one of the few who considers adoption, you need information, encouragement, and support.

- If someone you know considers an adoption plan for her child, she needs your support.

- You or someone you know may be adopted. You (and everyone else) should know that birthparents don't *want* to "give their baby away." It takes a great deal of love and courage to place one's child with another family through adoption.

• You may know adoptive parents—or you may adopt
  a child some day. You need to know the extremely
  important role the birthparents play in adoption.

Adoption Is Changing

Some people think placing one's baby for adoption
means the birthmother will never see him again. For a good
many years, this was true in agency adoptions and in most
independent adoptions. However, the practice of adoption
in the United States has changed a great deal in the past
decade. "Open" adoption is now possible in many areas.

Open adoption may mean the birthparent(s) and adoptive
parents exchange letters and pictures several times a year.
In many cases, the adoptive parents and the birthparents
meet before the baby is born and continue personal contact
after the adoption is finalized.

---

*The adoption decision cannot be made
until after the baby is born.*

The birthparents may choose the family they want for
their baby. Their adoption counselor may show them
several descriptions of possible adoptive couples, and they
choose the one they think would make the best parents.
Some adoption centers encourage the pregnant woman (and
her partner if possible) to interview several couples in
person before deciding who should parent the baby.

This may happen several weeks or even months before
the child is born, and the birthmother may spend time with
the chosen adoptive parents during her pregnancy. Sometimes she invites them to be in the delivery room when the
baby is born.

From a legal standpoint, the adoption decision cannot be
made until after the baby is born. The birthmother is under

absolutely no obligation to carry out her adoption plan. If, after she sees her baby, she decides to parent, she has as much right as any other mother to do so.

If you or another pregnant teen is interested in learning more about adoption, you/she should contact an adoption counselor. You might go to a licensed adoption agency or to an independent adoption center.

You can also learn about adoption by reading *Pregnant Too Soon: Adoption Is an Option* or *Open Adoption: A Caring Option* (1988: Morning Glory Press). In both books,

Birthmother with adoptive mother and their child.

teenage birthmothers share their stories and their reasons
for making the adoption decision.

Counseling Is Important

It's important that both the potential adoptive parents
and the birthparents receive counseling. Adoption is a crisis
for everyone involved. Discussing the various issues with
someone not directly involved often helps one deal with
those issues.

There should be no charge to the birthparent(s) for
counseling. This is usually included in the fee the adoptive
parents pay when they adopt a child. Their fee also covers
the legal costs, and may include prenatal and delivery
expenses for the birthmother.

In many states, it is also legal for the adoptive parents to
pay "necessary living expenses" for the birthmother during
at least the latter part of her pregnancy. It is **not** legal for
the adoptive parents to pay the birthparents a direct fee in
exchange for their baby. Babies are not for sale.

*Good counseling is extremely important
for all those involved in adoption planning.*

Some adoption agencies permit open records—the
adoptive parents and the birthparents meet each other and
may remain in touch after the adoption is finalized. Licensed agencies usually provide good counseling services
for both the birthparents and the adoptive parents.

Independent adoption may simply mean birthparents
choose an adoptive family. Then the adoptive family hires a
lawyer to handle the legal work. Many times in independent adoption no one receives much, if any, counseling.

More and more, however, independent adoption centers
are being set up to provide not only legal assistance in

adoption, but also the all-important counseling for birth and adoptive parents. To repeat, good counseling is extremely important for all those involved in adoption planning.

Father's Rights in Adoption

Adoption laws vary a great deal from state to state and from province to province. Generally the father, as well as the mother, must sign the adoption papers. In some states, the man named as the father may sign one of three legal documents:

Father's Legal Options

1. He can give his permission for the adoption to proceed.
2. He can deny that he is the father of the child.
3. He can formally give up all his rights to the child.

State laws vary as to what will be done if the named father refuses to sign anything. If he is assumed to be the father, and he won't sign adoption papers, the adoption may be delayed or denied.

Counseling for birthfathers is important too. If the birthmother is able to select the adoptive parents, she or her counselor might encourage the father to be involved in the process. If he has a chance to discuss his feelings, he may realize the adoption plan is a loving and caring choice, possibly the best choice for the birthparents as well as for the child.

Adoption Planning Is Difficult

Even considering an adoption plan takes courage. Many women bond with their baby during pregnancy. When the baby starts moving, s/he may suddenly become "real."

Making an adoption plan means looking into the future and carefully attempting to judge one's resources and capabilities for parenting. These are some of the questions a pregnant teen might ask herself as she considers her baby's future:

* Am I ready to be a parent 24 hours a day?
* Am I willing to be responsible for my child? Or am I relying on my parents for assistance? If so, have they agreed to provide the help I'm expecting?
* Do I have a realistic plan for supporting this child financially?

The questions could go on and on. The point is to look at one's choices, think of the good things and the bad things about each choice, and then make a decision.

Your Parents' Feelings

Your parents may have firm opinions about adoption. They may be absolutely opposed to adoption. Perhaps they say, "No child of ours will be given away." Or they may push adoption.

I was five months pregnant when his mom came over and begged me to give the baby up for adoption. I was crying and crying, and she wouldn't listen to a word I was saying. She said I was so immature, that I was just a little girl and didn't know what I was doing. My mom was real mad.

Kristin, pregnant at 15

It's hard for some parents to realize that the *birthparents* make the decision for or against adoption. Whatever their ages, this is the birthparents' decision. Parents of a 14-year-old parent-to-be may feel they should have a part in deciding whether this grandchild is to be part of their family or will be reared by a different family. It's a difficult time for them.

If you or someone you know is considering adoption, you might want to recommend that your/her parents read *Parents, Pregnant Teens, and the Adoption Option: Help for Families* (1989: Morning Glory Press). It's written for "birthgrandparents," those who may lose a grandchild through adoption. Others who have faced these decisions share their stories and their suggestions for coping.

Making the Final Decision

Sometimes the baby's mother and/or the father make an adoption plan during pregnancy, then change their minds in the hospital. When they see their baby, they feel instant love. How, then, can they possibly release this child to someone else to rear?

It's a good idea to write down the reasons for deciding on adoption.

It's best to stall a couple of days before either finalizing the adoption plan or deciding to parent the child themselves. After going through labor and delivery, the mother probably finds it hard to make this life-changing decision. At the moment, she "knows" she can't let her baby go.

If an adoption plan is made during pregnancy, it's a good idea to write down the reasons for deciding on adoption. Those reasons probably haven't changed now that the baby is born. If the mother (and father) can remind themselves of these reasons for adoption, they may be better able after delivery to make a decision with which they can live.

It's all right if they change their minds. The final adoption decision can't be made before delivery. In some states,

independent adoptions are not finalized until several
months to a year after the child is placed with the adoptive
family. The point is that deciding to place or not to place
one's child for adoption must not be done on the spur of the
moment. Either way, it's a terribly important decision for
the birthparents and for their child.

Elisa Marie considered adoption but decided to keep her
child to rear herself. She wonders if she made the right
decision:

> *When I told my grandmother, she didn't know I
> was so far along because I wasn't showing. She
> wanted me to get an abortion, but I couldn't. I talked
> to a counselor about open adoption, but I thought that
> would be too hard.*
>
> *When I saw other girls raising their babies, it
> looked easy. For me, though, it's too hard. If I were
> starting all over again, I might consider adoption.*
>
> Elisa Marie, 15 - Delila, 9 months

Birthparents Will Grieve

Placing a baby for adoption is undoubtedly one of the
hardest things anyone can do. Any birthparent who carries
out an adoption plan needs to realize that s/he will probably
grieve intensely for this child s/he already loves.

Birthparents should plan to continue seeing their counselor for awhile after their child is placed with the adoptive
parents. In fact, this is the time when counseling may be
especially needed. Joining a support group of young
birthparents may also be helpful.

Supporting an Adoption Plan

If someone in your class or another friend is considering
an adoption plan for her baby, what can you do to help her?

Things that are *not* helpful include saying:

- *How could you possibly give your baby away?*

- *You must not love your baby.*

- *No one who cares about her child would consider adoption.*

Why would anyone make such thoughtless comments? Saying these things would be very hurtful to a young person considering an adoption plan. Most often, people making these comments are simply thoughtless. They don't realize how hurtful they are to a person going through the pain of deciding how best to provide a satisfying life for her child.

Students in a class of pregnant teenagers were discussing adoption. "How can we support a student who considers this very difficult and unpopular decision?" asked the teacher. Lauren, pregnant at 17, replied with exceptional thoughtfulness and caring:

Listen and understand her thoughts. If someone tells you she's thinking about adoption, always listen with an open mind. Don't put her down for thinking that way because everyone has the right to their own thoughts. Maybe you don't agree, but it's not up to you. Understanding and listening is a lot of help in itself.

Deciding to let another family rear one's child is a tremendously difficult decision. For a pregnant teen not yet ready to parent, adoption may be the most loving choice. Having friends who support the young birthparent(s) throughout this difficult time is important.

Her baby will be born soon.

CHAPTER 7

PREPARING FOR LABOR AND DELIVERY

During the first few weeks of pregnancy, you were probably busy with all those decisions you had to make. Perhaps you had to deal with the emotional upheaval your pregnancy caused your family, your boyfriend, and yourself. At the same time, you've been coping with the many physical changes discussed in Chapter 2.

By the time you feel your baby moving inside you, you'll probably begin to think about labor and delivery. People may have shared their labor and delivery stories with you. Hearing other people's stories can be helpful, but remember that each person's experience is unique. While some mothers describe their baby's birth as a high point of life, others have more negative issues to discuss:

Labor was sort of easy for me. At 1 a.m. I started having pains, but they were small. They weren't that hard. Around 3 a.m. we went to the hospital. I was only dilated to two centimeters, so they sent me home.

At six that morning I had more contractions, and they really started hurting. Around 9 a.m. we went back to the hospital, and by then I was seven centimeters dilated.

My mom was my coach, and I held her hand. I felt like screaming, but I couldn't. I had my baby at 11, and then I fell asleep until 3 p.m. It wasn't so bad.

Miranda, 14 - Arianna, 4 months

My labor lasted two nights and a day. The first night they told me I wasn't in labor, I guess because my water bag didn't break. My contractions were already so strong I couldn't even move.

I went in at 2:30 a.m. and was dilated to three centimeters. The next day the doctor checked me and said he didn't want to induce me. They gave me a shot and sent me home.

The contractions stopped for a little while, and I fell asleep because I was so tired. The contractions came back, and that night my mom took me back to the hospital.

My husband and my mom were supposed to be my coaches, but they went to work about 4 a.m. the next morning. They didn't expect me to have the baby until that afternoon. At 5 a.m. my water bag broke. At 7:30 I was still only three centimeters, but at 8:30, I had her. I couldn't reach my husband, and by the time my mom got there, she was already born.

Lei, 16 - Keonia, 3 months

Nine Months of Preparation

Most of us want to know how we can have as good a birthing experience as possible. You can do a lot all through your pregnancy to help you and your baby work together to have the best possible birthing experience:

Stepping Stones to Labor and Delivery

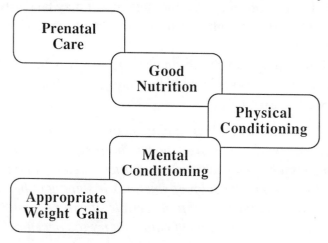

Early Contractions Possible

During the last few weeks of your pregnancy, your uterus will begin practicing for the big event.

Uterus: The hollow muscle in which your baby is growing

You may feel early contractions. A contraction feels like your uterus is making a fist. You can see your belly get hard and move as your baby pushes it.

These early contractions are called Braxton-Hicks contractions or *pre-term* or *false labor*. Sometimes people call them *pains*. Using this term, however, may make these sensations feel more like pain. The more you can relax and work with your baby now and when real labor begins, the less discomfort you're likely to feel.

When you get that first contraction, you may feel excited. You may even wonder if your baby will be born that

day. You're likely, however, to have false labor on and off
for several weeks.

While some moms report that they don't experience
these before-labor contractions, most do at least once or
twice. The discomfort many mothers report may be partly
related to getting uptight about this important work of their
uterus and baby.

Taking a prepared childbirth class generally helps.
Medication can also help with discomfort, and that's
discussed in Chapter 8.

*The prepared childbirth class helped me a lot. It
showed me what to expect, how to breathe, and how to
pace myself. And each time a contraction came, I con-
centrated on being calm. If you think it's going to be
horrible, and the pain will be terrible, it will be a lot
worse. If you keep yourself calm and try to concentrate,
it's not as painful or as hard.*

Delia, 16 - Kelsey, 7 months

Prepared Childbirth

Prepared childbirth means just what it says—preparing
for childbirth.

Prepared childbirth classes usually consist of a series of
meetings for parents-to-be. Purpose of the meetings is to
help the parents understand the process of labor and delivery. The mother and father, the mother and another helping
person, or the single mother by herself prepare for the birth
of the child.

Mothers and fathers who are prepared will understand
what is going on during labor and delivery. They will know
how to work with the contractions and the baby in order to
get the baby born as comfortably and safely as possible.

*Prepared childbirth was a help because I knew what
was going to happen, and it didn't scare me so much.*

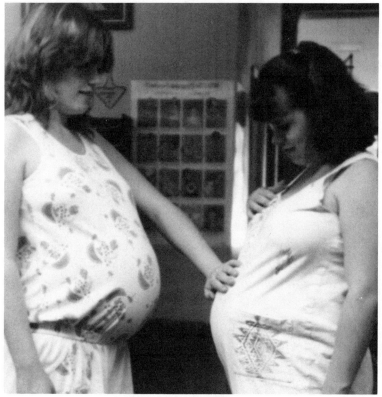

"Do you think that's a real contraction?"

It helped a lot with the breathing. Without it, I think I would have panicked.

Vicki, 17 - Deanne, 3 weeks

Prepared childbirth teaches you to concentrate on something so you won't scream. Women who hadn't had preparation were screaming and screaming, taking out IVs, taking out the fetal monitor, screaming at their husbands—it sounded like a mental hospital, not a delivery ward.

Theresa, 16 - Nick, 6 months

Check into the prepared childbirth classes in your area. You will be expected to take someone with you to your classes so that s/he can coach you during labor. Usually this person is the father of the baby.

If your baby's father either isn't around or he doesn't want to be involved in labor and delivery, ask someone else. Your mother, friend, even your father might make an excellent coach. The important point is that you get to a prepared childbirth class.

> *Prepared childbirth helped me a lot with focusing and breathing. Both my parents went into the delivery room with me.*
>
> *My dad wasn't going in but I said, "Put that suit on and go," and he did. They had never seen a birth before, and my dad was real nervous. After Antoine got here, Dad wanted to hold him so bad he could hardly let the nurse clean him up.*
>
> Elysha, pregnant at 17

The coach plays an important role in prepared childbirth. S/he knows what's going on in your labor, and will be able to coach (tell you what to do) so you can cope better with the whole process. Most hospitals now allow the coach to go into the delivery room with the mother.

> *The prepared childbirth class helped. It showed me what to expect, how to breathe, although I didn't use much of the breathing. Each time a contraction came, I concentrated on being calm. If you think it's going to be horrible and the pain will be terrible, that's when it's going to be worse. If you keep yourself calm and you try to concentrate, it's not as painful or as hard.*
>
> *Randy didn't take a class, but he watched programs on TV. He was there through delivery. I was in labor four days, and Randy would say, "Okay, calm down." He was my courage to go through it.*
>
> *He was real helpful with anything. He would help me get up from bed and walk me around. He was good*

about that. I was in active labor for four days, and I
ended up with an emergency C-section.

                                                    Delia

Prepared childbirth does not mean any one "method."
Any one of several different methods may be used. Neither
does prepared childbirth (sometimes called "natural"
childbirth) mean you must endure whatever happens without the help of anesthesia. With adequate preparation,
however, many women find they need very little help from
drugs during labor and delivery.

There are three especially important reasons for taking a
prepared childbirth class during pregnancy, according to
Mary Crowley, prepared childbirth teacher:

- The class will help you conquer the fear of labor and
  delivery.

- You will learn about your body and what happens
  throughout pregnancy and delivery.

- You'll be able to share your childbirth experience
  with someone else—the person you choose to be
  your coach.

"You'll also find you aren't out there all by yourself
being pregnant," Ms. Crowley commented. "You'll meet
other parents-to-be, and this is one place you can ask *all*
your questions about childbirth."

Prepared childbirth will help you understand
what's going on when you're going through labor
and delivery. My mom will be my coach. I feel better
about it now because I understand what will be
happening to me when my baby is born. My sister
can't believe I know so much about pregnancy. She
thinks I'm an expert.

                                    Marlene, 8 months pregnant

Relaxation Techniques Are Helpful

If you practice relaxation techniques at least twice each day, you can train yourself for labor. Remember, labor is just another name for work, and most of us need some training for a new job.

Some of these relaxation techniques are:

- **The Limp Noodle:** Tighten up all the muscles of your body and hold your breath for as long as you can. When you let your breath out, let go of all your muscles. Practice this two or three times each day for ten or fifteen minutes. You need to be able to do this automatically when you're in labor, and this will be hard if you haven't practiced.

- **The Focus Point:** Find something you like to look at (*not* a clock), something that you can see clearly from across the room. Look at it hard for a minute or two. At the same time, imagine your whole body is floating toward this *focus point*. Then take a deep breath and look away from the object. Try it again in five minutes or so. Focusing completely on something else can help you handle the discomfort of labor.

- **Breathing:** Practice a long breath in through your nose, out through your mouth. This provides a maximum amount of oxygen for your body.

- **Touch Transfer:** Have someone rub your back. At the same time, have that person tell you how good this feels. Feeling that person's hands on your back and hearing a soothing voice during labor will help you be more relaxed. Somehow you can mentally transfer at least some of the pain to that person's hands. Even firm hand squeezes can help with this process.

- **Pelvic rock:** Get down on the floor on your hands and knees. Arch your back up high like a cat. Then push your stomach toward the floor. Do this several times each day.

- **Kegels:** Kegels refer to the muscles you use when you urinate. Squeezing these muscles, then releasing them (as if you were going to start to urinate, then stop suddenly, then start again) helps prepare you for childbirth. Pretend you're in an elevator. Squeeze your way up to the tenth floor. Now come down again, stopping at every floor. Do this several times a day. You can also do your Kegels while you're urinating. Practice stopping or slowing down the flow of urine, then beginning again.

- **Walking:** Walking several blocks each day is good for all your muscles if you're wearing tennis shoes or other flat shoes. Going for a walk after lunch or dinner could mean less heartburn, too.

- **Situps:** Basic situps with knees bent are good, too. So is all basic stretching.

Labor Is an Athletic Event

Labor is an athletic event. Even if you haven't been into sports before, this is an event in which you will be the star. Just as athletes prepare every day, so should you do something daily to prepare your body and your mind for labor.

It will be an athletic event for you, but your prize will be a little different. Your prize will be your baby.

Be prepared!

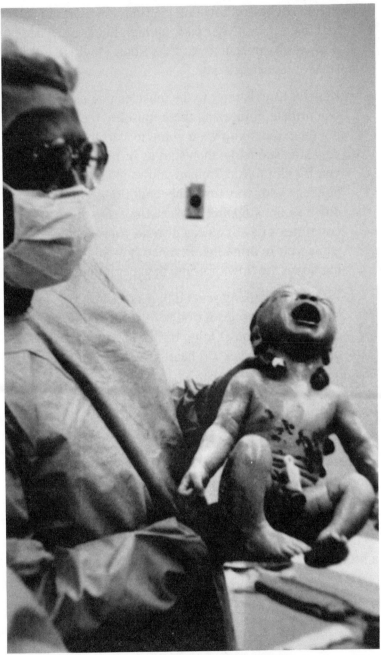

He's ready to face life on the outside.

CHAPTER 8

YOUR BABY IS BORN

My labor started at night. I couldn't sleep—about every 30 minutes I'd wake up and walk. I got up to go to school the next morning, but I wasn't feeling good, so I didn't go.

Later that day my contractions were getting closer. By 10 p.m., they came about every seven minutes. My mom said, "Do you want to go to the hospital?"

I said, "Not yet." Then I lay down, and the contractions came every five minutes. At midnight I told my dad to take me to the hospital. I could barely walk by then, and the nurse took me in a wheelchair to a room.

They put two belts on my stomach, one to measure the heartbeat of the baby, and one for the contractions.

The contractions got stronger, and two hours later,
I had Duwayne. It didn't hurt as much as I expected.

Shalonda, 16 - Duwayne, two months

Hint: Ask your doctor at what point during these signs of early labor s/he wants you to call. What should you do if you go into labor when the office isn't open?

Signs of Early Labor

Labor may be easier for you if you understand what is happening inside your body. Your uterus has several jobs to do before your baby is born. One of these jobs is the softening of your cervix.

Cervix: neck of your uterus

When you're not pregnant, your cervix is usually tightly closed. This is the reason your baby doesn't fall out during pregnancy.

As labor begins, your body releases hormones which tell your cervix to soften up and get out of the way. This process is referred to as *dilation*.

Dilation: opening

Both your vagina and your cervix become soft and stretchy during labor. This makes it possible for your baby to come out.

During pregnancy, your cervix is sealed with a mucous plug. This plug keeps germs in the vagina from getting in the uterus, germs which could give your baby an infection. During labor, this plug comes out. It will be stringy, gooey, and white with possibly a tinge of pink. This may be your first sign of labor. When it happens, call your doctor.

Some people never notice the mucous plug. Their labor may begin with the rupture of the sack of amniotic water. This is the sack in which your baby has been growing.

If this happens, you'll feel a gush of warm water. If it's amniotic fluid, it will keep coming out no matter how much you try to hold it.

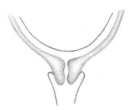

Beginning dilation
(Not active labor)

Dan went in with me although we never took Lamaze classes together. I only had a three-hour labor, but it was real hard labor the whole time.

My water bag broke, and the next thing I knew, we were on our way to the hospital. It was at night, and I was almost three weeks overdue.

When I first saw her, I was happy. Then I got hungry.

Cathi, 18 when Susie was born

Mid-labor
(Regular contractions)

Other people have back-aches and feel "heavy" when labor begins. Practicing your prepared childbirth techniques during this time will be helpful.

End of labor
(Your baby is ready for birth)

Timing Your Contractions

When your contractions start, have someone time them.
How far apart are they? Count the time from the beginning
of one contraction to the beginning of the next contraction.
This is the *interval.*

How long do they continue? Count the time from the
beginning of the contraction to the end of it. This is the
duration.

If this is real labor, your contractions won't go away.
Your doctor will want to know both the interval and
duration of your contractions.

Fetal Monitor

Soon after you arrive at the hospital and are settled in the
labor room, the nurse will place a fetal monitor low on your
stomach. The fetal monitor is a device for measuring how
long, how hard, and how often contractions come. It also
keeps track of the baby's pulse and breathing. It looks like
a paddle, and is fastened on with a belt. It doesn't hurt.

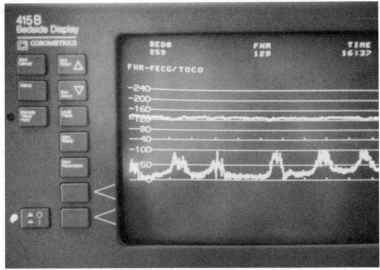

This is what you'll see on the fetal monitor screen.

Pain Relief Medication

You may also want to talk to your doctor about pain relief during labor. Find out about your choices *before* your labor begins. Even if you're sure you don't want drugs during labor and/or delivery, you should know about your options. It's easier to understand your choices when you're not already in labor. With or without medication, you can expect a fine healthy baby.

The principal medication offered to mothers in labor is a form of morphine called demerol. Demerol is given either through the IV or with a shot to your hip.

IV (Intravenous): Method of giving medicine
by inserting a needle into the vein,
usually in the arm.

Demerol can dull some of the pain, but it also goes through the placenta to the baby. It may cause the baby to become sleepy, and it can slow labor down. You may want to ask your doctor if s/he uses this drug or any others during labor.

The most commonly used anesthesia is the epidural. This is a process in which the doctor places a soft rubber catheter in the lower back. A medication similar to what a dentist uses to lessen dental pain is then injected. This causes numbness from below the umbilicus (bellybutton) down into the legs.

I was at the mall shopping for furniture. All of a sudden I felt this sharp pain that felt different, and then I felt wet. I went to the bathroom and checked. I wasn't sure it was my waterbag because it was a very slow leak. Then I started feeling contractions, but I wasn't sure I was in labor.

*My mother was with me, and we decided to go to
the hospital. I thought they might send me home, but
they said, "We'll keep you. You're in labor." And
within half an hour, I had gone through transition. I
was in labor a total of four hours. He was already
crowning when I got to the delivery room.*

*I had an epidural. Once those pains started com-
ing, I turned into a real baby. If you don't like pain,
the epidural is wonderful. I was able to enjoy everything. I got an episiotomy which didn't hurt until the
epidural wore off.*

Courtney, 15 - Ricky, 3 months

If you have this kind of medicine, you'll need to stay in a
lying down position for a few hours after delivery. Usually
this isn't difficult since you'll probably be pretty tired
anyway.

*I started getting the pains Saturday night, about 15
to 20 minutes apart. By 11 p.m. they started coming
three to five minutes apart. We went to the hospital at
midnight, but I was only dilated three centimeters.
About 1:15 the doctor broke my water bag.*

*The contractions were coming faster and harder.
At 3:30 they gave me a shot of demerol and I felt a lot
better. The demerol wore off in a couple of hours, and
the contractions were closer and harder than ever
and hurting even more.*

*Finally they gave me some more demerol. They
checked me at 7:15 a.m., and I was dilated to a little
more than nine centimeters. The next thing I knew the
doctor gave me a shot to numb me for my episiotomy.
Then they told me to push.*

*I pushed for about ten minutes, and I heard my
baby crying. My aunt was saying, "He's so pretty.*

Look at all his hair." He didn't look too pretty
though. He was all purple.

They cleaned him up and brought him back to me. I
fell in love like never before. He had the fattest little
cheeks and so much hair, and his thumb was in his
mouth.

Alice Ann, 15 - Vincent, 3 weeks

Transition Stage

The last period of labor is called *transition*. This begins
when the cervix is fully dilated. During this period the baby
moves down into the birth canal and prepares to come out.
When the head of the baby can be seen, it is described as
crowning—what a lovely word! Someone important is
coming—your baby.

If you're going to deliver in a delivery room, this is the
time you'll be taken there. If you'll be in a birthing room,
your doctor or midwife will stay with you now until your
baby is born.

When the doctor or midwife decides it's time, s/he'll tell
you to push when you feel the urge to do so. This feeling is
the same as the urge to have a bowel movement. Pushing
too soon can cause the cervix to swell and slow things
down. It also puts more pressure on your baby's head.

It usually takes less than five pushes to bring your baby
into the world. Many mothers say this is the most exciting
part of the whole process. At the very least, you know that
your labor is ending.

I didn't go into labor by myself. When I was nine
months, my doctor said, "Let's wait another week."
Two weeks later he decided to induce my labor, and I
was so scared.

My mom and Carlos were there the whole time.
First I'd squeeze Carlos' hand, then my mom's.

When I was three centimeters, my doctor asked if I wanted pain medication. All through my pregnancy I had said I wouldn't have anything, but now I told him I wanted the strongest thing he had.

He gave me an epidural, and I was out for two hours. Then I started feeling everything again. The contractions were coming and coming and coming. I was in labor for 23 hours.

I was eight centimeters, and I wanted to push, but the nurse kept saying, "You can't push yet." I wanted to push so bad, but if I had, I guess the cervix would have swelled, and it would have been even harder.

Finally she told me to push. I was pushing and thinking, "Oh my God, this thing is never coming out." But I pushed once, and that's all it took. Elena came out.

Monica, pregnant at 14

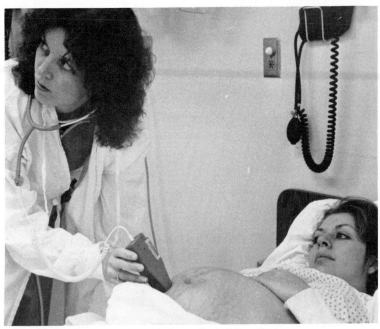

"Yes, she's really in labor."

As the time for delivery gets nearer, the doctor may perform an episiotomy.

Episiotomy: a small cut made
to enlarge the vaginal opening

Not all women need the extra opening, but sometimes doctors make it to avoid the possibility of having the tissue tear. It's a little like having a seam split on your clothes. It's much easier to fix a straight seam than an irregular tear.

If you've had medication injected, you won't feel this cut. Actually, you may not feel it even if you don't have medication. Nature provides some numbness in this area.

Finally—The Delivery Room

When you arrive in the delivery room, you'll be placed on a table similar to an operating table. You'll be in a position like the one needed for a pelvic examination.

You may feel shivery, and they'll put warm blankets over your legs and body. It isn't really cold, it's just a hormonal shift that prepares you for the most exciting part of this adventure.

If you want to watch, be sure to tell the nurse/doctor to adjust the mirror for you. If you wear glasses, you may want to request them. I (Jeanne L.) missed seeing the birth of one of my children because I wasn't wearing my glasses. I simply couldn't see in the mirror clearly.

After you're in position, the doctor will wash the birthing area. Your baby's progress will be watched carefully, and they will be checking your baby's heart rate often. Don't be alarmed by this concern. It's all part of making sure things are going well for both of you.

The crowning is part of the baby's descent from your body into her own world. The head slips out of your body and turns to the side. (Some films about delivery make it look like the doctor turns the head, but it's the baby who turns.) The shoulders now come out one at a time. When the second shoulder comes out, the rest of the body emerges quickly. This all takes less than five minutes!

This ends the second stage of labor. Your baby is born.

> *I didn't feel Vincent come out. They told me to push, and then they said, "Oh, look at all his hair." I was so tired, but after he was born, I wasn't tired at all. My aunt had said, "As soon as you see the baby, the tiredness goes away." And it did.*
>
> *They brought him to me wrapped in a towel after they cleaned him up, and he was sucking his thumb already.*
>
> Alice Ann

Usually you'll see your baby right away. You'll feel lots of excitement as you find out the gender and condition of your new person. Some babies cry immediately, and some need to have mucous or amniotic fluid removed before they begin to cry. The nurse will gently remove the mucous and amniotic fluid with a bulb syringe.

> *I got to see Keonia right after she was pulled out. They put her on my belly for a little while before she was taken to be cleaned up. She was long and skinny and was better looking than I had expected. She was warm, wet, slippery, and there was a smell—not a bad scent at all. To me, it was a sweet scent.*
>
> Lei, 16 - Keonia, 4 months

Delivery of the Placenta

Next on the agenda is your body's completion of the birth process. The placenta has nourished your baby for nearly nine months. It now needs to end its service by separating from your uterine wall and coming out. This happens within 15 minutes of delivery. One or two menstrual-like cramps and out it comes.

Your doctor will then repair your episiotomy by putting in a few stitches. Large sanitary napkins are put on you. You will have very heavy period-like flow of blood for a few days. Occasionally a blood clot will come out too. These are from the area where the placenta separated from the uterus. Unless the bleeding is bright red, you don't need to worry about it.

During this flow time *do **not** use tampons*. The tissue is so soft the tampon could go up quite high in the vagina and you'd have a problem getting it out. An infection could then develop and cause you to be quite sick.

You may go to a recovery room if you have had anesthesia. Or you may go to a regular room for the few remaining hours you'll spend at the hospital.

For Some, a C-Section

For about twenty percent of moms, a Caesarean section is necessary.

Caesarean section (C-section): Delivery of child by cutting through walls of abdomen.

Delia was in that twenty percent needing a C-section. Her labor didn't progress as she expected:

About 11 a.m. I started to get contractions. They were every three minutes, and they came out of the blue. They were in my back, then would come to my front. I was at home by myself with my little brother, and our phone was disconnected. I had to go across the street and call my mother. She had a friend take me to the hospital.

*They checked me, and the contractions got stron-
ger and stronger—two minutes apart. My doctor
checked me. He said I wasn't dilating yet, and my
waterbag hadn't broken, so he said we had to stop the
labor. He gave me a shot, and the contractions
slowed down and weren't as bad.*

*He checked me at 6:30 p.m. that day and said I still
hadn't started to dilate. A little later my contractions
got real bad again. Another doctor checked me and
said I still wasn't in active labor, and that I should go
home. So I went home at midnight.*

*The next morning the contractions kept coming,
and they were strong. At 10 a.m. I had finished taking
a shower, and I was dressed. I was blow-drying my
hair when all of a sudden all this water gushed down
my legs. I thought, "God, am I wetting myself without
feeling it?"*

*So I changed my clothes and put on another pair of
pants. It happened again. So they rushed me to the
hospital, but by that time, my contractions had
stopped.*

*They started again soon so I called Randy and
said, "This is it." He rushed over to the hospital, and
he was all happy. My contractions were strong, and
the nurse made me walk around for a couple of hours.*

Kelsey started to cry immediately when they lifted her out.

---

*Then I checked into the Birthing Center, but I still
wasn't dilating. They started shooting stuff into me,
and within an hour my contractions were so painful
and so close I could barely catch my breath
between them.*

The nurse came in and rushed me to the other side of the hospital. The doctor said my baby was in danger, and he had to do a C-section. They gave me an epidural, and I started feeling better. Kelsey started to cry immediately when they lifted her out.

I started to shake, and my temperature went up to 104°. I stayed awake just long enough to see Randy holding Kelsey and saying, "I've got a daughter. I've got a daughter."

Delia, 16 - Kelsey, 7 months.

Being told during labor that she must have a C-section is usually disappointing to a young woman. Liz shares her experience:

When he said I had to have a C-section, I broke out in tears. I was scared. I didn't want one.

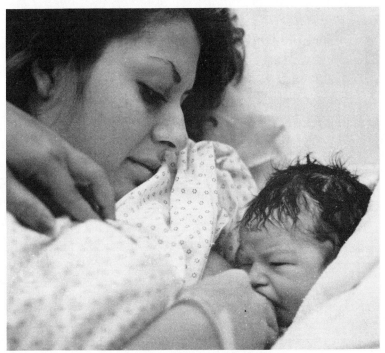

Mother and baby get acquainted.

*First they put the IV in, and they got me all
prepped and ready. They shaved my stomach including the top pubic hair. Then when they moved me to
the delivery room they put the epidural in my back.*

*I couldn't feel them cut, but when they pulled her
out I could feel it. I'm lying there and have a curtain
in front of me. I heard him cry, and my mom said,
"It's a boy."*

*And I said, "Does he have all of his fingers and
toes?"*

*Then I asked the nurse what his Apgar score was,
and she said, "What do you want it to be?"*

I said "Ten."

She said, "How about 9.9?"

It happened so fast.

*I was so tired I couldn't even keep my eyes open. I
hadn't slept for a long time. I stayed in the hospital
for four days, and I healed pretty fast. I was sitting up
and walking around the next day. But when I came
home, I was real tired.*

Liz, 16 - Jonathan, 3 months

Other reasons a mom might have a C-section include:

1) Cephalopelvic disproportion—the baby is too big in
comparison with the mother's size

2) Labor slows down or stops

3) Certain types of infections

4) Placenta previa (placenta covers inner cervix)

5) Fetal distress

6) Breech (bottom first) or transverse (sideways)
position of the baby

Doctors used to feel that when a mom had one C-section,
all her later babies would have to be delivered that way too.

Now we know that if the condition that caused the first C-section isn't present during a later pregnancy, she may be able to deliver vaginally.

Baby's First Test

Your baby's responses will be measured and noted with something called the *Apgar score* at the time of his birth, and again after a few minutes. Scores range from 0 to 10. Most babies have scores between 6 and 9.

The Apgar test measures the color, pulse, cry, movements and strength of breathing. If comments are made about these things by the doctor and nurse, don't feel worried. It's normal for them to be watchful.

Your baby will be weighed and measured, washed, and wrapped in a blanket. The nurse will then either take your baby to the nursery or give her back to you for a few minutes, depending on the practice of the hospital.

Going home is something fathers often find an especially exciting event. Maybe they feel fatherly responsibility around that time. Being in charge of mom and baby makes them more aware of their part in this new life.

For each of you, going home is the beginning of your new adventure.

When we came home I felt different. This was something new. I had to start my life all over again, learning who comes first, and trying to get all the sleep I could. I had to get used to another person, a very loud person you can't ignore, somebody I had to attend to the minute he opened his mouth. My life was changed forever.

Elysha, 21 - Antoine, 4

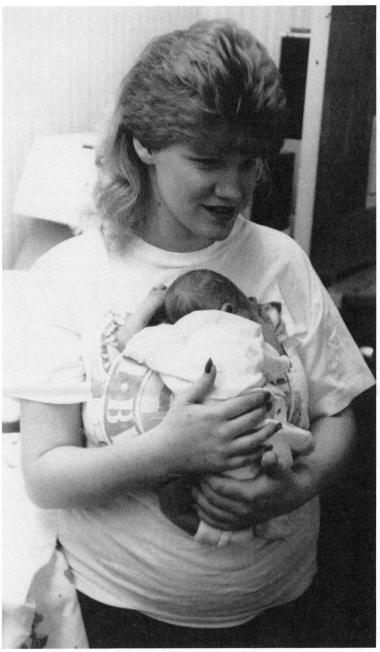

Your fourth trimester—and baby is finally here.

CHAPTER 9

YOUR
FOURTH TRIMESTER

I didn't really want to go home from the hospital.
I guess I felt more secure there—I was scared. When
I did go home, I wasn't sure what I'd do with him.
I was all by myself that first day. Orlando just ate and
slept, so we stayed in bed all day.

Holly, 17 - Orlando, 5 months

You may be surprised at how easily you get tired during
the first few days after you deliver your baby. Your fatigue
is a combination of the after-effects of labor, your lack of
sleep because of your baby's frequent feeding, and the
hormonal changes your body experiences after delivery.

Remember the tiredness of early pregnancy that was
caused by hormone changes? Now those hormones are
changing back.

Your stitches may hurt for a few days. You'll be having some bleeding for about two weeks. Use napkins rather than tampons to care for the bleeding after delivery, as explained in Chapter 8.

It's a good idea to continue taking your prenatal vitamins, especially if you're breastfeeding. This will help you avoid anemia and speed your recovery.

You may notice changes in your temperature as your hormones change gears. If you feel sick as well, be sure to check your temperature. Sometimes a mom has an infection and needs to call the doctor.

I'm happy that I had a baby. I wanted one, but during that first week I said, "Oh God, I shouldn't have had this baby." But after the first week, Joe started helping. And I suppose it was after-baby blues, too.

Rosita, 18 - Jenny, 4 weeks

Don't get upset when he cries. Andrea used to hate it. If Dennis cried for a whole minute, she'd be crying, too.

That first day she was trying to change him, get him dressed, feed him—and he wouldn't shut up for anything.

Ted, 18 - Dennis, 2 months

After-Baby Blues

A lot of mothers are unhappy at least part of the time during these first few weeks. To make things worse, a young mother may think she *should* be delighted—this baby for whom she waited so long is finally here. So why isn't she thrilled?

I had 19 hours of labor, so I was exhausted. I held Karl while they sewed me up, and while they rolled us back to the nursery.

I didn't see him again until the next morning. I think the hospital was too strict. They would bring him in every three or four hours. All I could do the rest of the time was look at him through the nursery window. That wasn't very satisfying.

Because I didn't see much of Karl in the hospital, I wasn't prepared for the crying when we got home. He cried all night at first, and I didn't have enough sense to sleep when he did during the day. I had all these things to do, so when he slept, I'd work furiously. But then he would keep me up all night. I was miserable.

Kimberly, 17 - Karl, 2 months

Because so many mothers get these unhappy feelings after childbirth, doctors give the condition a name—Post-Partum Depression or after-baby blues. Realizing how much work a baby takes and how tied down she is with this tiny helpless creature are two of the reasons she feels sad. But she also has a physical reason—her body is adjusting to being non-pregnant. As your hormones work hard to "get over" your nine months of pregnancy, you may feel pretty mixed up at times.

Each time Elaine cried, I cried. Not being able to get back in my clothes bothered me, too. I was pretty depressed from the day I came home with Elaine until she was about three months old. Then I started being a little happier, calmer about things. I was only 16 then. With Susan, I haven't had much depression.

Maya, 21 - Elaine, 5; Susan, 7 weeks

I would think about everything—the father, how is it going to be for Patty as she grows older if she doesn't have a father? Sometimes I would cry, and I didn't know why.

Beth, 18 - Patty, 3 weeks

Getting Help

Today was a rough day. She's been a grouch the whole day. Last night she was even worse. I try feeding her, changing her, singing to her, and nothing seems to work. I just don't understand what she needs.

Sometimes I feel like I'm going crazy. I think I need time to myself because I haven't had that in awhile. These past few days have been hard. I haven't gotten anything done. I don't even have time for my work.

Marlene, 15 - Evan, three weeks

The best cure for after-baby blues is to get some help with baby care and to take some time to do things you want to do for yourself. If you can get away from the house, go to the mall or a movie for a couple of hours. You'll feel much better.

Mother needs to sleep when baby does.

I (Jean B.) remember my mother advising me to sleep when my baby slept, and that really helped me. It also helps a lot to talk to someone. Don't keep those unhappy feelings all bottled up!

Remember, too, that you can get help for many problems. You are entitled to finish school. You can get food stamps and financial aid if you're eligible. Call your teacher, doctor, nurse or social worker to find out about job training, daycare services, church programs, social programs, or other support opportunities in your community.

If you have just had a baby, and you feel sad even as you look at your beautiful infant, remember that you're not weird. You're perfectly normal, and you'll probably feel better soon.

Life-Style Changes

Often a teenage mother—any mother and most fathers, for that matter—finds caring for a tiny baby changes her style of living a great deal.

> *I can't do the things I used to do like go to the beach. I have to stay home with the baby. I'm not as free as I used to be. I have to wash clothes and make formula. I don't get as many calls from my friends as I used to. That bothers me. I like to shop and I can't go shopping as much. I'm not dating because I have to be with Chandra all the time.*
>
> *Sometimes I want to go someplace. I get ready to go, and then . . . suddenly I see the baby there beside me. I've just forgotten her!*
>
> Maria, 18 - Chandra, 6 weeks

As your baby matures, you'll be able to include her in some of your activities. Life may never again be quite as

simple and carefree for you—no more deciding on the spur
of the moment to take off for the beach or the river. Even
shopping with a small child is complicated. But with extra
planning, it can be done.

*My life style is entirely different. Before, I could
just get up and leave and do things on instinct. But
now we have to plan ahead and take about an hour
getting ready to go. You plan your life, too—she's
with you so your life has to be different. Especially
money—you can't just be spending your money on
anything you want now.*

                                        Cheryl, 16 - Racquelle, 8 weeks

*My girlfriends used to ask me to go with them.
They used to call me when he was about two weeks
old, and they'd say, "Let's go out and have a good
time."*

*I'd say, "I can't because I have to take care of
Eric." They called again and again for about a
month, but then they stopped. They knew I couldn't go
out with them.*

*They come over to see me, and they talk about
parties and stuff. Then they look at me and say, "I'm
sorry," because they're talking about it in front of me.
But I don't mind. When Eric's older, he can go with
me some places if there isn't drinking and pot.*

                                        Jeanne, 16 - Eric, 2 months

Bonding with Your Baby

Bonding with your baby means falling in love. It has all
the same ups and downs about it. Anybody who has ever
fallen in love with anyone knows there are times when the
person you love the most can make you terribly angry as
well as lift your spirits remarkably. This can be true of
your baby.

Sometime during the first two months you should feel this surge of love, that this baby is truly yours. Some people experience these feelings more strongly than others. If a mother's life isn't going as well as she'd like, she may not bond as easily with her baby.

Feeding your baby yourself, holding your baby, talking with other people about your beautiful child, and showing your baby off to others all help this falling-in-love-with-your-baby phenomenon.

Handling Stress

It's all right if sometimes your baby makes you feel angry and frustrated. It's all right that some mothers sometimes want to run away from home.

All mothers (and fathers) need to learn ways of dealing with this stress. Sometimes it means someone else giving you a break. It may mean leaving the housework and going to visit a friend for a change of pace. Sometimes it may mean calling a hot line. Every mother is going to have these feelings at least occasionally.

> *I remember nights when I just wanted to go crazy because I didn't know what to do.*
>
> *Being alone is hard. I used to wish that Norm had just half the responsibility—just to let him have a baby for a week, for a night. But of course I would never do that. It was hard. It's hard to remember now the times I stayed up at night and just pulled my hair and wanted to run away. I'm at home with the baby most of the time now.*
>
> Julie, 16 - Sonja, 7 months

Teen moms are often reluctant to ask their fathers to baby-sit, but sometimes a grandfather is a fine person to watch the baby. It gives him a feeling of participating and helping his daughter through a difficult time. It gives him a way to involve himself.

Take a Few Minutes Off

If you start feeling tense and uptight, and you have no one else to take care of the baby, what can you do? Sometimes it's better to put her in her crib where you know she's safe, then walk away from her for a short time. This may be better for baby than if you try to cope with more than you can handle right now.

You may need to get out of the house. Go out in the back yard and walk around. Or run around in circles until you feel the stress go. Some moms find that exercising helps them relieve tension.

You can go back to doing prenatal exercises and other relaxation techniques you learned during pregnancy without hurting yourself or your stitches. More vigorous exercising should be delayed until all bleeding has stopped. If you feel lightheaded, you should stop and rest awhile.

> *There are times when you just want to spank her butt so hard. What I've done a few times is lay Sonja down and take a walk. There have been a couple of times at 2 a.m. when I couldn't do anything with her, so I'd lay her down and walk around the block—even though it's not the safest neighborhood in the world.*
>
> Julie

Don't feel guilty about it. Sometimes mothers do that. They know they have to get away, but they still feel guilty. It's okay. It may be necessary occasionally, especially for a single parent who can't poke a father in the back and say, "It's your turn."

Of course you should never leave your baby alone in an empty house. Julie, who mentioned walking around the block in the middle of the night, lived with her parents. Because they were home, she could leave occasionally when she was upset.

A mother living alone might ask her next-door neighbor to stay with her baby for a short time when she needs to get away. If you need to get out for awhile, find a way to do so.

Your Partner Relationship

Many young women, and many young men, too, wonder what sex will be like after their baby is born. Some moms are not in a relationship that includes sexual intercourse, but others are. Guys sometimes wonder how long you have to wait, while moms are more worried about whether it will hurt, or if they even want to do it. Actually, you may be so tired those first weeks after delivery that sex doesn't even sound interesting.

It's important that you have a checkup before you begin to have intercourse after childbirth. The first time or two the tissue may still be tender, and each partner needs to be patient with the other.

The vaginal opening will be about the same size it was before you ever had sex. At first, hormonal juices that help keep the area moist may not be working too well. Therefore, a lubricant such as KY jelly or the jellies sold for contraceptive purposes will help.

At any rate, this is a topic you and your partner should talk about *before* your baby is born. That way both of you will understand what to expect.

The two of you can also be making a decision about the kind of family planning you'll use. Remember that you could begin to ovulate as soon as two weeks after you deliver—which means you could get pregnant again. See Chapter 14 for more information about family planning, a *very* important topic for new parents.

Breastfeeding—a beautiful experience for mother and baby.

CHAPTER 10

FEEDING YOUR NEWBORN

I breastfed Dennis the first two months, and I'm glad I did. I think it was worth it because it was more convenient then. I also felt closer to him. That's probably why he slept so much and was such a good baby. But I changed to formula recently mostly for my own convenience. With summer here, I wanted a little more freedom. And I wanted Ted to be able to feed him.

Andrea, 17 - Dennis, 3 months

Many Choose Breastfeeding

More and more young mothers are choosing to breast-feed their babies. Perhaps they've been told it's best for the baby. They feel they "owe" their baby the best care possible. For them, this includes breastfeeding.

*I didn't give Karl any formula for at least a month.
He was completely breastfed. I stopped because I was
going to work. Mostly I liked breastfeeding. I felt I
was doing a little more for him, that I was giving him
something directly from me.*

Kimberly, 17 - Karl, 2 months

It's also perfectly all right to choose this method because
it's easier for the mom. Having no bottles to sterilize, no
formula to mix, and no heating required can make life
much simpler for a tired new mother. And, of course,
breastfeeding is cheaper. That's good news for the
pocketbook, too.

*It's really handy. When I go places, I pump be-
cause I almost always use breast milk. I've tried
formula once in awhile, but Patty spits it up. I'm
breastfeeding because they say it's good for the baby.
But it's also handy and saves money. You don't have
to get up and heat the bottle. That's when I especially
like it.*

*Patty wasn't a very good nurser. I wondered if she
was getting enough, but she was. My breasts didn't
get very sore, just a little. They gave me stuff at the
hospital to put on them, and that helped.*

Beth, 18 - Patty, 3 weeks

*It's so easy. We didn't have to drag bottles and
milk along when we went camping.*

Alison, 18 - Stevie, 3 months

Erin, whose first son was born seven years ago when she
was 16, now has a nine-month old son. She described her
breastfeeding experiences with the two children:

*I wanted to breastfeed Kelton. I thought I was
doing it wrong, but I wasn't. He wanted to eat every
two or three hours, but I thought he should be on a*

four-hour schedule. I figured maybe he wasn't getting enough to eat. (Grandmother: *We were afraid we were starving him.*) *I had enough milk, I'm sure, but I thought he should just eat every four hours, so I switched to bottles.*

I'm breastfeeding this one completely. I finally found out they want to eat every two or three hours because they digest breast milk faster. Right now I'm trying to wean Wayne to a cup.

Breastfeeding is so much cheaper. Do you know how much that formula costs? You're also supposed to lose weight while you're breastfeeding, and it makes you rest. That's good.

I wish I had known with Kelton, but he wanted to eat every two or three hours and we were on that strict schedule. Dumb! You're supposed to feed them every 2 to 21/2 hours because each time they nurse, it stimulates the breast to produce more. I really recommend breastfeeding for anybody.

Erin, 23 - Kelton, 7; Wayne, 9 months

Breastfeeding Takes Effort

Breastfeeding her first baby hasn't been easy for Holly, but she insists it's worth the effort:

I had problems at first. Orlando constantly wanted to suck, and my nipples were getting sore. My mom kept telling me I was running out of milk. She couldn't breastfeed her own kids, so she seems to be totally against it. I thought about trying a bottle, but Orlando is a breast baby. He loves it, and I do too. He's already 41/2 months old, and he won't take a bottle at all. He really should so I could get out once in awhile. But within two or three months he'll be able to drink some milk from a cup.

He loves to breastfeed. I tried a pacifier when my nipples were sore at first, but he didn't like that. Then he started sucking his thumb and that helped.

Holly, 17 - Orlando, 5 months

Stevie slept a lot the first couple of weeks, but the breastfeeding was hard at first. He wanted to eat constantly. He nursed at least once every hour or two. My nipples didn't get sore, which surprised my mom. I think it was because I massaged them and tried to get ready for nursing while I was still pregnant.

I'd try to feed him, but sometimes those first two weeks I'd get nervous, and the milk wouldn't come. This made him feel worse, of course. So we bought a can of formula, and he drank some of that. I got more milk, perhaps because I relaxed and quit worrying about him starving.

Some people say you shouldn't offer formula until after breastfeeding is going okay, but this worked for us. Soon I could satisfy him with just breastfeeding. He still hasn't finished that first can of formula. I'd nurse him first, then offer him formula if he still seemed hungry.

Alison

If Alison had offered the formula first, she probably wouldn't still be breastfeeding. The more the baby sucks, the more milk one's body produces. It made sense to feed him formula if he was still hungry *after* nursing. He had already, through his sucking, "told" her body to produce more milk for next time.

However, for a good start with breastfeeding, it's probably best not to give the baby a bottle during the first month. This gives your breasts and your baby a chance to get well started with breastfeeding. Remember, your breasts create more milk only if stimulated by baby's

Breastfeeding intensifies bonding between mom and baby.

nursing—or if you express milk (squeeze out) by hand or with a breast pump.

After the first few weeks, it's a good idea to give the baby a bottle occasionally so she'll know how to suck from

one. There may be an emergency sometime when you can't
be there. This will also give grandma and dad a chance to
feed the baby.

Breastfed babies don't need additional water. Of course,
it's okay to give her plain water if she appears to want it.

Mom's good health is an important part of breastfeeding.
Continue taking your prenatal vitamins. You still need the
same foods you needed for a healthy pregnancy. Your
weight will return to normal gradually, and even faster
when you breastfeed.

If your baby seems fussy or appears to have gas, think
about what you ate the day before. If you had a lot of any
one food, or if you added something new, it might be
affecting your baby. Cut back or eliminate that food and
see if baby is happier.

Is there a La Leche League chapter in your community?
La Leche League is an organization of breastfeeding
mothers. A local group will usually have a series of several
meetings dealing with the how-to of breastfeeding.
Members are available to help each other find answers to
questions or problems with breastfeeding.

Check your telephone directory. If you find the League
listed, you can call to learn of meetings of possible interest
to you. If you have problems with breastfeeding, you can
usually get help by calling their number. Maternity ward
nurses and lactation specialists can also help you.

To read more about breastfeeding, see *Bestfeeding:
Getting Breastfeeding Right for You* by Mary Renfrew,
Chloe Fisher, and Suzanne Arms (1990: Celestial Arts).

Breastfeed in Public?

Obviously breastfeeding is the natural way to feed a
baby. Since babies have a habit of getting hungry no matter
where they are, ideally mother and baby "should" feel
comfortable nursing almost anywhere. Surely most people

Breastfeeding in public can be managed nicely.

would agree that when baby is hungry she should be fed.

In some areas, however, breastfeeding is not often done in public places—a custom which can make life hard for a hungry baby and her mother if they don't happen to be home at mealtime.

Sometimes mothers choose to bottle feed because they think they would have to stay home to breastfeed the baby. Many mothers, however, feel comfortable throwing a blanket completely over the baby while she nurses. Usually, people assume she's asleep.

One time we were at Mike's baseball game, and I went to the car to feed Eric. When Mike and his friends came back, I had him all covered up with a blanket while I nursed him. They said, "Sh-h, he's asleep." I smiled and nodded.

Jeanne, 16 - Eric, 2 months

Getting Started

The breasts don't contain real milk for two or three days after delivery. Instead, they produce "colostrum." This is a yellowish substance which contains water, some sugar, minerals, and many important antibodies. This gives the baby some protection against illness. Even a few days of breastfeeding will give your newborn a good start.

The more often you nurse your baby,
the more milk your breasts will produce.

If a newborn baby is hungry, he will turn his head toward a gentle touch of your finger or nipple on his cheek. This is called the rooting reflex. As he turns his head, his lips will get ready to suck, a reflex action all ready to go at birth.

When you're ready to nurse baby, hold him and touch the cheek next to your breast. He'll turn to suck. You can help by holding your nipple between your fingers so baby's nose isn't buried in your breast. Be sure he gets as much as possible of the areola (dark area around the nipple) into his mouth as he sucks.

Just two or three minutes on each side are enough the first day. Gradually increase the time. Within a week your baby will probably nurse three to five minutes on each side. If your baby still seems hungry, you can offer a small amount of formula by bottle. If she doesn't seem hungry, but still wants to suck, offer her a pacifier. Babies need lots of sucking.

If you offer the left breast first at one feeding, start with the right one the next time so that baby will empty each one completely. This is important so that your breasts will "know" to produce more milk on both sides.

The more often you nurse your baby, the more milk your breasts will produce. Be careful not to let your nipples get too sore those first few days. If your nipples get sore, keep them dry and expose them to air. Putting pure lanolin on them may make them feel better.

If your breasts get hard and uncomfortable, nurse your baby and/or express (squeeze out) the milk. You can freeze this milk for later use as needed. A warm shower and breast massage may also help.

If milk leaks from your breasts between feedings, you can use purchased pads to protect your clothes. Probably more effective are pads you can make yourself. Cut a cloth diaper into small pieces about three inches square. Sew several layers together, then put in your bra as needed. They're easily washed.

Burp your baby after he finishes nursing at each breast. Just hold him up to your shoulder and rub his back gently. He probably won't burp as much as he would if he took a bottle. Breastfed babies don't usually swallow as much air as bottle-fed babies.

Breastfed babies tend to be ill less often during their first year.

Another very important reason to choose breastfeeding is the fact that breastfed babies tend to be ill less often during their first year of life than are bottle-fed babies. A breastfed baby is less likely to catch a cold, for example. Have you ever cared for a tiny baby who couldn't breathe because he couldn't blow his nose? If so, you know how hard it is for both mother and baby.

I know how much easier breastfeeding is for me compared to my mom's friend. She had a baby about the same time I had Stevie, and she's bottle-feeding

*him. He's had three colds already, and Stevie's had
none. Her baby cries a lot, too.*
Alison

Of course, breastfeeding your baby doesn't guarantee no
colds for a year. And if you bottle-feed, you aren't guaran-
teed a certain number of colds! All we know is that
breastfed babies are *less likely* to get sick than are their
bottle-fed friends. They are also less likely to develop
allergies.

With these facts in mind, make your own decision. If
you prefer to bottle-feed your baby, fine. Above all, *don't*
feel guilty. You certainly can be a "good" mother, no
matter which feeding method you choose.

If, while you're pregnant, all of this seems confusing,
perhaps you simply will decide not to decide. If you
breastfeed baby for just a few days, he'll get the colostrum.
If you then decide you don't like breastfeeding, switch to
bottles with a clear conscience.

*I breastfed Danette for a couple of months, but I
didn't care for it. I was leaking through everything,
and it just wasn't for me.*

*It was neat being close to her, but I didn't really
like it. I prefer bottles myself. Every time I wanted to
go out, I would miss one of her feedings. My breasts
would hurt so bad.*
Caroline, 18 - Danette, 10 months

Some Prefer Bottle Feeding

Lots of babies do great on carefully measured, carefully
sterilized formula. To learn how to make formula, simply
follow the directions found in every package/can of prepared formula. If baby is lovingly held while he drinks his
bottle, he probably feels about as good emotionally as he
would if he were breastfed.

I decided on bottle feeding mostly because of the time—and because my mother bottle-fed all of her babies. I tried breastfeeding in the hospital, and I didn't like it. I wish I hadn't bothered. Sterilizing the bottles doesn't take much time. My sister and my brother sometimes feed her. I use pre-mixed formula—no mixing to do.

Vicki, 17 - Deanna, 3 weeks

Check the size of the nipple holes occasionally. They should be just big enough so that milk drips slowly from the bottle when you hold it upside down.

If the milk comes out too fast, the holes are too big. He won't get enough sucking as he drinks. The only solution is to buy new nipples.

If the holes are too small, you can enlarge them. Dip a needle in boiling water, then stick it through the nipple holes to make them bigger.

I decided to bottle-feed Jonita, but when she was about two weeks old, I was still leaking. My friend talked me into breastfeeding her then. I did for about a week, but that didn't work out. If I had it to do over, I think I would breastfeed because I felt really close to her that week. It was neat.

Ellen, 17 - Jonita, 61/2 months

Whether you breastfeed or feed your baby with a bottle, eating time can be a period of special closeness for the two of you. Talk to her as she eats. Tell her how much you love her. Let her know how much you like this part of your day, and she will respond more and more as the days go by.

A baby being held and fed by a loving, unhurried parent is learning that most important lesson—to trust her world and you.

Cherish the time you have together.

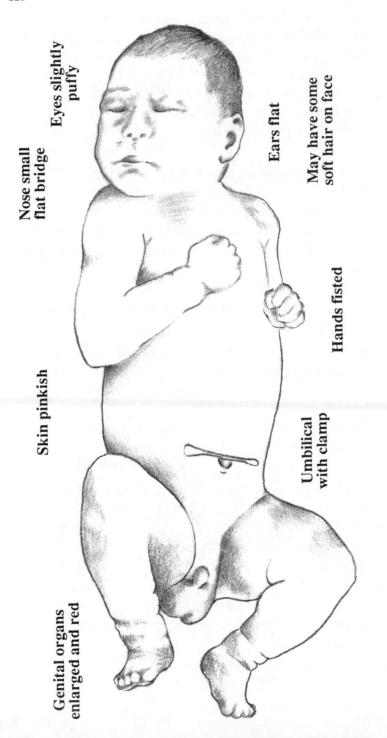

Eyes slightly
puffy

Ears flat

May have some
soft hair on face

Nose small
flat bridge

Hands fisted

Skin pinkish

Umbilical
with clamp

Genital organs
enlarged and red

CHAPTER **11**

WHAT DOES A NEW BABY DO?

Labor is called labor because it's such hard work for the mother. It's also hard on baby. A just-born baby doesn't look at all like the charming little person in the diaper commercials. Instead, she may look red, wrinkled, and worried.

When I first saw Patty, I thought, "Golly, was that inside me for nine months?" She didn't look very pretty—too white and awfully tiny. But the doctor said her color would come soon, and it did.
Beth, 18 - Patty, 3 weeks

Nearly every mother, father, and grandparent, however, will swear she is the most beautiful baby ever born:

It was instant love . . . but still it was hard to believe Dennis was here, that what was inside of me

*was now a little baby. I thought he was cute. What I
liked best was his little neck—he didn't have any!*

                                    Andrea, 16 - Dennis, 2½ months

What Does She Look Like?

Most babies look pretty messy after delivery until the
nurse cleans them up. Often a baby's head becomes *molded*
during labor and delivery. Instead of looking round like
most people's heads, hers seems longer than it should.
Sometimes there are bumps and lumps on her head too.

*At first I thought Dennis was ugly. He had a big
lump on his head right in front, but it was down the
next day.*

                                    Ted, 19, Dennis' father

At birth, the bones in baby's head are soft enough to
change shape slightly in order to go through the birth canal.
Within a few days baby's head will become round. If her
mother is in labor a long time, baby's head is more likely to
undergo molding.

Regardless of their ethnic origin, most babies are fairly
red when they're born, sometimes even purplish looking.
By the time she goes home from the hospital, her skin will
look better. When she cries, her skin may turn red and
blotchy. This, too, is normal.

Black babies' skin is often lighter at birth than it will be
later. The skin at the tip of the ear is a good indication of
the baby's permanent color.

*When Racquelle came out, I said, "She's all
purple!" Her head was shaped a little funny because
they used forceps. She was all messy. They held her
up and let me kiss her. I almost started crying—it's a
real good feeling you get.*

                                    Cheryl, 16 - Racquelle, 2 months

Babies have a "soft spot," actually more than one, on the top of their heads. This is also called the fontanel.

Some people are afraid of the soft spot. They think baby might be injured if the soft spot is touched. However, this spot is covered with a tough membrane which gives plenty of protection.

The skull doesn't close over the soft spot for about 18 months. During that time, it's important to wash the baby's head thoroughly to prevent cradle cap. Cradle cap is similar to heavy dandruff. When you give your baby a shampoo, just massage her head with your finger tips as you would your own. Touching the soft spot is not going to hurt it.

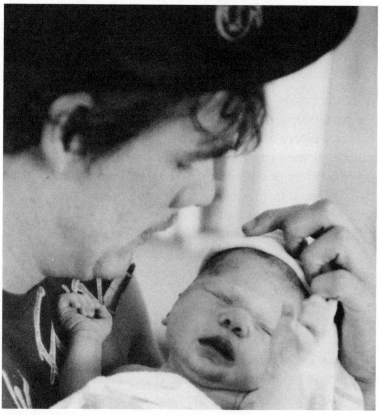

Dad and baby get acquainted.

If cradle cap does develop, the best way to treat it is to wash baby's head with a low-allergy soap or clean her head with a soft brush.

Bellybutton Care

Newborn babies have a couple of inches of umbilical cord still attached to their navels. This cord turns black and usually drops off within a week. Most doctors suggest that baby not be put in water until after the cord drops off because the area needs to dry out. Sometimes the area bleeds a little those first few days. It can be cleaned gently with cotton dipped in alcohol.

> *Today Evan's bellybutton cord fell off. I went to change him and I found it stuck to his diaper. I'm glad it came off because I thought it was ugly.*
>
> Brandy, 15 - Evan, one week

Some babies' bellybuttons stick out more than usual. In the past, people often put snug belly binders on their babies—pieces of cloth wrapped firmly around the baby's middle. Sometimes people put tape over the navel or even taped a penny or other flat item over it. They thought this would keep it from sticking out. Actually, it won't help, and it can cause irritation.

If baby's bellybutton sticks out, it sticks out. That's all right. This condition usually disappears sometime during childhood. If it sticks out a lot, however, ask your doctor to check for umbilical hernia.

How Baby Develops

If you know something about your baby's development, you'll find him more interesting. If you think he's interesting, you'll give him more attention. Give him more attention, he'll respond more to you. A beautiful circle to enter!

Of course all babies are different. Even at birth, your baby will look different than other babies in the hospital nursery. He may cry a lot, or he may be quiet much of the time. Most babies sleep a great deal the first weeks, but yours may stay awake several hours a day. Accept him as he is and love him.

A newborn human is far more helpless than is a new kitten, colt, or other baby animal. He depends completely on his parents or other caregivers for survival.

She's able to lift her head off the bed for a few seconds when she's lying on her stomach, long enough to keep her from smothering in a soft mattress.

In fact, a baby can't smother by lying face down in a bed with no pillows. When she needs air, she can turn her head enough to get it.

Babies usually respond to sounds at birth. She will startle at a loud noise, perhaps cry.

She can hear rather well. Of course she doesn't understand your words, but she likes the sound of your loving voice. After all, during the last few months before birth, she was "hearing" your voice, or at least feeling the rhythm of it, while she was in your uterus. Now it's important to talk and sing to her. Loud sharp noises and angry voices will upset her, but she loves your gentle voice.

When I change Sonja's diaper, I always talk to her and play with her. I talk to her when I feed her, too. She always likes that.

Julie, 16 - Sonja, 7 months

What Can He See?

He can't see well when he's born. The world probably looks hazy to him. He can see objects best which are about nine inches from his eyes. When he's breastfeeding, this is about the distance between his and his mother's eyes.

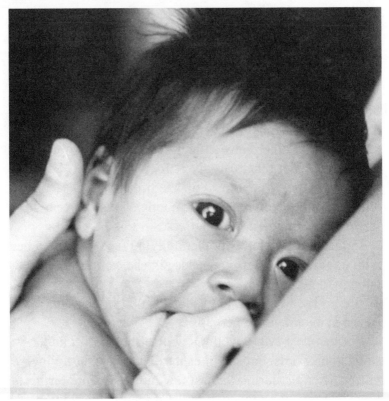

He doesn't see very well yet.

Sometimes parents worry about their newborn's eyes. They seem hazy, and sometimes even appear to be crossed. The baby can't focus well yet because nerve connections between his brain and eye muscles aren't complete. His vision and control will develop gradually, and soon his eyes will stay put.

At birth, most babies' eyes are dark blue or gray. Their eyes will gradually change to their permanent coloring. Some dark-skinned infants are born with dark brown eyes.

Sometime between birth and six weeks of age, most babies can begin to follow an object for a short distance with their eyes. You can easily "test" this ability with your baby.

— Test Baby's Vision —

Use a big object with strong contrasting tones. A piece of cardboard that is at least five inches across and has black and white squares on it works well. Choose a time when your baby is awake and comfortable. Hold the cardboard about 12 inches from his eyes. Move it slowly from one side to the other. Do his eyes follow? For how long?

At first, he may show interest for only a few seconds. By the time he is two or three months old, he may watch the item as it moves all the way from one side of his head to the other.

Her favorite "object" is your face. She may look at you with interest almost from birth. Sometime between birth and about two months of age, she will smile at you. It's an exciting milestone.

In the past, experts insisted that if a new baby looked like she was smiling, it was not a real smile. True, her smile may be partly a reflex, but it usually happens when she is content. An awake baby begins to smile in response to someone at around one month.

Suggestion: Since your newborn is most interested in looking at faces, make her a "face" for her crib. The simplest way is to draw colorful features on a paper plate. Tape the plate to the side of the crib about ten inches from her head. Choose the side of the crib toward which she most often looks.

A non-glass crib mirror or a picture of you would be fun for baby, too. Before long, she will enjoy looking at her reflection.

Notice Her Reflex Actions

Baby's behavior at birth is mostly reflex action.

Reflex action: Responding to something
without having to learn to do so.

Rooting and sucking are reflex actions. While a newborn
usually needs some help in finding the nipple, he generally
knows how to suck once he gets there.

A new baby is not quiet, even when he's not crying. He
will hiccup, startle, and shake because his nervous system
is still immature. This is not a problem. Sometimes,
however, a young mother needs reassurance:

> *Once I got scared because Nick started shaking
> and making weird sounds after I fed him. It was
> 1 a.m., and I woke Paul up. He said Nick had the
> hiccups, so I relaxed.*
>
> Theresa, 16 - Nick, 6 months

Another reflex action exhibited by a newborn baby is the
"walking" reflex. If you hold him upright with his feet just
touching a firm surface, he will take "steps." He will
actually place one foot in front of another while you support his weight. This lasts only a week or so. Then if you
hold him upright, he will simply sag rather than making
walking movements.

Baby's hands are almost always clenched into fists
during the first month or two. This, too, is a reflex action.
If you put your finger in his fist and pull back gently, you'll
find surprising strength in that little fist.

Those First Days

The main thing you may notice about your newborn is
her sleepiness. During her first days of life "outside," she
will probably be alert only about three minutes per hour on

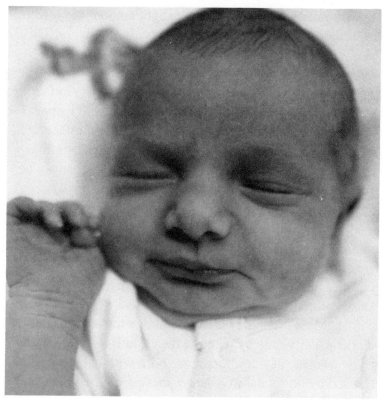

Most newborns sleep a lot those first few days.

the average. She will be even less alert at night (you hope).
This "alert" time is in addition to the time baby spends
crying because she's hungry, wet, generally uncomfortable,
or lonely, and the time she spends eating.

All babies lose a few ounces during the first two or three
days after birth. This is perfectly normal. Baby will gain it
all back within a few days.

Babies, both boys and girls, sometimes have swollen
breasts for a few days after delivery. This is caused by the
hormones in the mother's body. Sometimes the baby's
breast will contain a little milk. This is called witch's milk
in some cultures. This is normal and will go away within a
few days.

Girl babies sometimes have a slight amount of bleeding from the vagina for two or three days after delivery. This, too, is caused by mother's hormones. It's nothing to worry about.

Newborn boys often have very large testicles. In fact, both boys and girls have oversized genitals which appear swollen and red at birth. These are also caused by the mother's hormones. They will become smaller within a couple of weeks. A boy baby may get an erect penis when you change him. This normally occurs occasionally throughout infancy and early childhood.

Baby may have birthmarks. Some of these will disappear in time. "Strawberry" marks and dark moles, however, generally stay on baby for life. These marks tend to run in families, and you can do nothing to make them go away. Dark colored marks may also be on Black or Hispanic babies. Most often they are on or above the buttocks. These marks usually fade by the time the child is two years old.

Newborns may develop or are born with baby acne. Caused by hormonal imbalance, these are little white heads that will disappear in a couple of weeks. No treatment is needed.

Observe Him Closely

If the baby becomes too warm, she may develop miliaria. These are little whiteheads on the surface of the skin, usually on the nose and cheeks. To prevent them, don't overdress your baby. Babies need about the same amount of clothing that you need. This does *not* mean wrapping her in a warm blanket on a hot summer day!

Thirty to fifty percent of all full-term and eighty percent of premature babies develop jaundice which causes their skin or the whites of their eyes to get yellowish. There are several causes, most of which have to do with the baby's immaturity. Should your baby look yellowish, check with the doctor. Extra blood tests will be given, and the treatment could be as simple as giving her more water to drink. Occasionally, special lights may be used to get rid of the yellow skin color.

Baby's bowel movements are worth watching. New babies have greenish BMs that are softer than those of an adult. If color, texture, and odor are normal, the number doesn't matter much. A breastfed baby will usually have a yellowish BM every time she nurses. That's because a

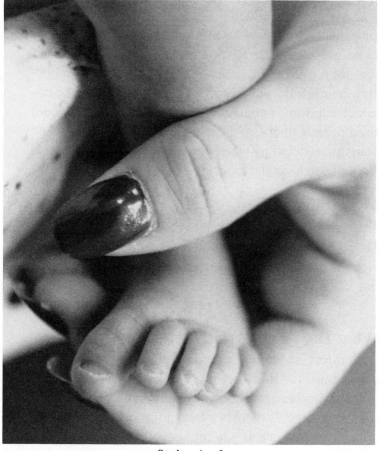

Such a tiny foot. . .

breastfed baby digests the milk faster than does a bottle-fed baby. This is good for her.

The first bowel movement a baby has after birth is called meconium. Meconium is a greenish-black sticky substance which fills the intestines of babies before they're born. Almost all babies pass meconium during the first day, sometimes for three or four days. Ted, a young father, commented, "Those black poops freaked me out!"

The Circumcision Decision

Some boy babies are circumcised soon after birth. This is an operation in which the loose folds of skin at the end of the penis are removed by the doctor.

Before a baby can be circumcised, parents must sign a consent form. Before delivery, parents should decide, if they have a boy, whether or not they want him to be circumcised. Some people feel it's easier to clean a circumcised penis. Others say it is an unnecessary operation. Sometimes deciding whether or not to have a son circumcised depends on the family's ethnic and/or cultural background.

Some parents decide to circumcise or not to circumcise depending on whether the father has had this operation. They think their son might be more comfortable if he looked like his father. Others think it is important for their son to look like the other boys around him. If most boys are being circumcised, he will be too.

What Does Baby Want Out of Life?

Comfort is the most important thing to a newborn. She is a very sensitive little creature.

Your newborn will probably startle and cry at any sudden change. If there is a loud noise or if her bassinet is jolted, she may cry. If you lift her suddenly from her bed, she may cry.

When you pick her up she will feel more secure if you put your hands carefully under her, then wait a second or two before you lift her. She'll then have time to adjust to being moved. Of course you *always* provide head support for a young baby when you lift or hold her.

> *That first month was not what I expected. I thought taking care of Chandra would be easy, but it was hard. When she cried I thought I could just pick her up and she'd go to sleep right away. But she didn't.*
>
> *It was more work than I expected. I had to fix her milk, change her diapers—I didn't think she'd be wet* **all** *the time. She had to be changed constantly. I'd be watching TV, and I'd hear her crying. I'd get kind of mad because I didn't want to move.*
>
> Maria, 18 - Chandra, 6 weeks

Comfort first of all means having her needs met. Letting her "cry it out" makes sense only when you can't do anything to help her feel better. Even then, most babies prefer to be held in their misery.

Nearly every baby loves to be touched, held, and cuddled. They have a way of snuggling into your arms that makes both you and baby feel good. When baby is fussy, holding her upright with her head near your shoulder may quiet her.

Infants Don't "Spoil"

Most parents, if they let themselves go, love holding their baby. Touch her, love her. Above all, don't worry about spoiling her in these early months.

Most experienced mothers and other child development experts agree that babies under six months of age don't cry because they're spoiled. We're sure of this because we know babies don't develop a memory until late in the first year.

Young parents often ask, "If I pick her up when she cries, won't she think she can get whatever she wants by crying?" This old idea simply isn't true. Yes, she'll cry when she needs something, and she will learn something from the parent who answers her cries. She'll learn a basic sense of trust in her world. And that sense of trust is the most important thing she can learn during her first months.

I talked to my great-grandmother before she died (before I was pregnant), and she said, "I never let any of my babies cry. Whenever a baby cries, it has a

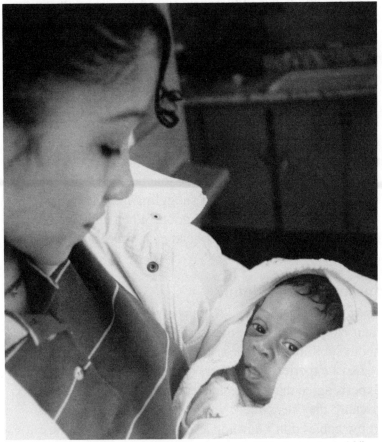

"Whenever a baby cries, it has a need, even if it's just to be held."

need, even if it's just to be held." So that was stuck in my head.

So when Sonja was little, if she cried, I fed her. If she cried and wanted to be picked up, I picked her up. My mom would tell me I would spoil her. She was eating every two hours until she was about 2 1/2 months old.

Julie

Sometimes Paul will lie there for a long time and look around after he eats. He really gets upset only when he's wet. He hates lying on his back—he cries and screams and hollers. The hospital told me to put him on his side, but that didn't make too much sense. He would roll right back over to his back, and then he would cry more.

We feed him when he cries. He wakes up every three or four hours, sometimes in 2 1/2 hours. My mom thinks I should feed him every time he moves.

Deanna, 16 - Paul, 3 weeks

By the way, research shows that babies who are picked up often during their first months cry *less* at one year of age than do the children who weren't picked up when, as infants, they cried.

So hold your baby. Pick her up when she cries. Feed her if she's hungry. (See Chapter 10, "Feeding Your Newborn.") Change her if she's wet or messy. Keep her clean, dry, warm (but not too warm), and fed.

Perhaps She's Lonely

When Chandra gets uncomfortable, she just cries and cries, and I don't know what to do. My mom works so she's not here during the day to advise me.

Maria

If she's not hungry, perhaps she's uncomfortable for another reason. Does she need changing? Was she burped enough at her last feeding? Is she perhaps too warm? Or is she too cold?

If nothing seems to work, perhaps she's lonely. Have you ever thought about what it must be like to be able to do nothing except lie in a bassinet by yourself? For nine months, you've been carried securely in your mother's uterus, then suddenly you're outside. And you're expected to sleep by yourself with no human contact. That's quite a change for your baby!

Perhaps she simply wants to be held. Do you have a rocking chair? Use it! A rocking cradle is also nice for a baby. Sing to her as you rock her.

I love rocking Stevie. The one thing my mother insisted on buying before he was born was that rocking chair, and now I know why.

Alison, 18 - Stevie, 21/2 months

If money for baby things is limited, your baby would undoubtedly rather you'd buy a cheap unpainted or used crib *and* a rocking chair, rather than just a fancy crib.

Babies like to be held close. Our friend, when her baby cries, sets him way out on her knees and bounces him up and down. He just cries harder because he doesn't like it. Poor little baby, I feel so sorry for him.

When Stevie cries, we pick him up and hold him close and love him. I think that's pretty important instead of sticking him out there on your knees.

Alison

He May Like Swaddling

Sometimes swaddling helps a fussy baby. This practice of wrapping baby tightly in a blanket is common in many cultures. After being somewhat cramped before birth, baby may feel more secure if she is wrapped snugly.

To swaddle a baby, center her on the blanket with her head just over one edge. Pick up an upper corner of the blanket and bring it down diagonally over her shoulder. Her elbow will be inside, but one hand should be free. Tuck the corner under baby's knees.

Pull up the other side of the blanket and fold it snugly over baby. Lift her a little so you can put the edge of the blanket under her.

You'll have a snugly wrapped baby, and you may have a more contented baby. In fact, some infants will sleep better if they're swaddled as they're put to bed.

Be Sensitive to Her Needs

Incidentally, when Stevie is asleep, we let him sleep. A lot of people don't realize this. I've seen friends wake their babies up just because they have company.

I think it's important to pick him up when he cries. Or if he's awake and not crying and you want to pick him up, fine. But not when he's sleeping. It's just as important to let him sleep as it is to pick him up when he cries.

Alison

Your newborn infant is a very interesting person who knows more than we used to realize. This is when you begin to be a big influence on your child's behavior. The kind of home you have and the things you do are important to your baby.

You have an exciting challenge as you care for her, teach her, and love her.

Dad and baby bond together.

CHAPTER 12

ESPECIALLY FOR DAD

If you're a teen father—or you're going to be one soon—what about you? As you probably know, many people think teen fathers don't care about their babies. They think teen fathers only want to make as many girls pregnant as possible, then forget about their responsibilities to those young women and the children they bear.

Of course many teen fathers aren't like that at all. You probably aren't or you wouldn't be reading this book.

You may be living with your baby's mother. You may be married, although only one in three teenage mothers is married to the father of her baby at the time of birth.

Perhaps you aren't living together but you spend a great deal of time at her house, and you expect to spend more after your baby is born. You may not have planned to be a father so soon, but you intend to parent this child together.

It was on Thanksgiving Day. She phoned me and told me she was pregnant. At first I figured, "Maybe she just thinks she is. How could I get somebody pregnant?" Then I got to thinking. Was it mine or somebody else's? You know, all that.

I used to go around doing whatever I wanted to do. Then I started realizing she was pregnant with my kid, and I started caring more and more. When she started showing, I felt there was a little of me in there along with a little of her. That's a good feeling.

My friends would say, "You're going to be a father?" They was cool about it. One of my buddies said, "Man, you ain't going to have no money. Every-thing you make is going for this kid." But everybody else wanted to be the godfather.

I'm supposed to graduate in four months, and I want to go in the Air Force. We'll get married after she graduates two years from now.

I want to be all the way involved with my baby. My kid is going to come first before anybody.

Norm, 17 (LaTisha, 15 - 9 months pregnant)

If You Aren't Together

You and your baby's mother may not be together. Perhaps you split up even before she knew she was preg-nant, but you still want to see your baby. You're still his father whatever your relationship with his mother. Miguel was in this situation:

I had just gotten out of jail when Maurine got pregnant. I wanted to straighten up, but I really didn't have feelings for anybody, and I wanted to mess around.

I didn't know for two months, and we weren't together then. When I found out, I thought, "I've got

*to do something. This is my first child, and I'm not
going to abandon him." I didn't want my child to
grow up not knowing me.*

*Finally we got back together about a month before
Genny was born. Before that, I felt like I did something wrong. I felt guilty, because if I had known she
was pregnant I wouldn't have messed around with
anybody else. I would have stayed with Maurine. I
wasn't mad at her.*

*I went with Maurine to the hospital, and that's the
best thing you can ever see, your child being born.
We didn't live together, but I started keeping Genny
on weekends. I was working, and I would take care
of her. I liked that. I had never done anything like
that before.*

*Maurine and Genny started living with me a couple
of months later, and I'd get up with Genny at least
half the time. We lived together for nearly a year, but
then they moved back with Maurine's folks. I still see
a lot of Genny, and I'd like to live with them again.*

Miguel, 19 - Genny, 18 months

Father's Rights

If Maurine should decide she doesn't want Miguel to
see Genny, what are his rights?

If the baby's father is providing some financial
support—and usually even if he's not—he has a right to
see his baby. Legally, he may be able to have his child with
him part of the time. If the young parents disagree on this
matter, they should talk to a lawyer or legal aid group.

If your partner doesn't want you to see your baby, you
need to do something about it, according to Julie Vetica,
teacher of a parenting class for young fathers at El Camino
High School, La Mirada, California. "Fathers have a right

to see their child, and sometimes they need to take the initiative rather than waiting around for their rights to fall out of the sky," she commented.

Ms. Vetica encourages young fathers to keep a record of their visits with their childen and to get written receipts for the money they provide for child support. This information could help if you ever need to prove in court your interest in your child.

Esteban and Trudy were both 15 when they realized Trudy was pregnant. At first, Esteban tried to avoid the issue of his approaching fatherhood. At the same time, he didn't want to desert his child as his father had deserted him and his mother:

It was a shock to me. I didn't want to be a father. I was too young. I thought we was just playing around, and all at once Trudy came up with something real serious. She lived around the block from me, and I tried to avoid her.

I ran away from it for awhile, but then I went back to her. My dad left when I was born, and I didn't want that for my baby.

I went out with other girls all through Trudy's pregnancy. I figured after the baby was born I'd have to settle down with this one chick, so I wanted to date while I could.

Trudy was moody, always snapping. She was scared too, but she didn't pressure me. I kept telling her I wasn't going to leave her, but I never told her why I was never home when she called.

I wasn't with her in the hospital because her dad don't like me. I didn't see Nathan until he was a week old. I used to hang out on the streets a lot while Trudy was pregnant, but after he was born I changed. When I saw my kid, how he looked like me, I calmed down.

Fulfilling your role as father is very special.

I dropped out of school because we didn't have any money. I got a job, but then I started back to school last fall. Next month I'm going back on independent study because we need more money. I have to go back to work.

Esteban, 18 - Nathan, 2; Ralph, 5 months

Her Parents May Reject You

Even if you have a job, your partner's parents may not want you around. The parents of many teenage mothers have little use for their grandchild's father. They blame him for their daughter's too quick shift from being a carefree teenager to a hardworking mother.

We were pretty close, her parents and I. Then when they found out she was pregnant, they had anger for me. I wasn't wanted in their house. Now that the baby is born, they seem pretty happy, and they like me again.

It really puts you down when they reject you, and that's what they were doing. But I stuck in there because in my heart I wanted to be with my son or daughter. I used to say to Darlene, "I understand why they feel like that, but why don't they give us a chance?"

                          Manual, 18 - Juan, 27 months; Darcy, 13 months

Pregnant teenagers tend to grow up fast. The physical changes they're experiencing seem to help them realize they are indeed facing great changes in their lives. If a partner is not closely involved, it's hard for him to understand. If he is involved, he may still find it difficult to cope with her moodiness. She may not be as much fun to be with as she was before she became pregnant. As her pregnancy progresses, she may focus more and more on her baby.

Don and I were real close, and he was happy I was pregnant. He'd always say stuff like he was going to spoil me and the baby, he couldn't wait, etc. He'd call to see how I was. We broke up when I was four months pregnant because I'd never go out with him. Don said I was grouchy and no fun any more.

                                    Liz, 15 - Jonathan, 3 months

Most parents would probably have a hard time feeling positive toward this young man. He's responsible for their daughter's pregnancy, yet he complains because she's "no fun any more." In fact, Liz' parents are determined that neither Liz nor her baby will ever see Don again.

Your Parents' Reaction

Sometimes it's the young man's family who is most upset about the pregnancy. Becoming a father too soon can damage their son's chances of reaching his career goals. This is not what they wanted for him. Some parents, although disappointed, will provide extra support for their son at this time, knowing that this is the best way to help him become independent as soon as possible.

After Deborah got the pregnancy test, we were real scared because she was a cheerleader and she wanted to go to all the football games that year. And I didn't expect to be a father. We considered abortion. I wasn't ready for this.

Then Deborah said she was going to have the baby with or without me. If I wasn't willing to go through with it, I could go home and forget her. That was too much guilt for me to handle.

I talked to my mom. She said Deborah could move in because she wasn't getting along with her mom. We ditched school for a few days, and my mom had a fit.

She said if we did that, Deborah had to move back home. She said we both had to get jobs and go to school, and we had to keep the house clean. I've been working after school at a meat market since that time. Deborah's working too. She had planned to go to college, but that won't be for awhile.

Nathaniel, 18 - (Deborah, 17 - eight months pregnant)

It's important that you do all you can to support your family financially. You probably need to get a job as soon as possible. Continuing your education, however, is also extremely important.

Your Responsibilities as a Father

If you're a teenager, you may find it difficult to "take your responsibilities" as a father. If you haven't finished high school, or even if you have, finding a good job isn't easy. The unemployment rate among teenage men is high.

If you're not working, people around you may think you don't want to be responsible for your child. If you've dropped out of school, it's even easier for them to write you off as a typical teen father, someone who will force his baby's mother to rely on welfare for financial support.

Legally, any man who fathers a child is expected to provide at least half the money needed to care for that child until s/he is 18. That's a scary thought for a teenager with no job. Taking that responsibility at age 15—or even 18— may be impossible.

If you realize how much it costs to support a baby, you may feel like giving up. Many young fathers do. They can't get a good enough job to take care of their families by themselves, so they provide little or no help. When we consider the money part of being a father, it's no wonder so many teenage fathers walk away.

Norm explained why he didn't do that:

> *Babies are expensive, but it's like, well, instead of me getting a pair of shoes, I'll give my baby this. I can't see why guys, when they have kids, don't get involved. I see the babies with their moms and I wonder, "How can you have a kid in this world and not want it?" It's a part of you. I couldn't have my kid running around without me being involved.*
>
> Norm

Don't Drop Out!

Esteban, quoted earlier, had dropped out of school when he learned Trudy was pregnant. He returned to school, but is planning now to drop out again because they need more money. He feels he has to get a full-time job.

That's a hard decision. Dropping out of school will probably mean Esteban won't be able to get a well-paying job. In fact, without even a high school diploma, he may

Your caring support means a lot to her.

never make enough money to support his family as he'd like. If he must go to work, he'd be wise at least to enroll in his school's Independent or Work Study program.

Esteban also needs to get some good career counseling. Perhaps his school has a career center where he can learn about job training. Some intensive job training now would help him avoid being stuck in a job with no future.

Shaun had his high school diploma and was enrolled in college when he learned he'd be a father soon. With help from his parents, he's continuing his education. He figures this is the most responsible thing he can do for his family at this time:

> *I was shocked at the pregnancy test. I cried with her. For a couple of weeks you can't think. I was in college and knew I wanted to stay there. That was a priority. I'd have a baby to take care of, and I had to get through college. I hoped my parents would understand and help me, and they've been pretty wonderful.*
>
> *I figured if I didn't stay in school, there wouldn't be many good jobs I could get. I could work at some job with no advancement opportunities. I decided I'd rather struggle the next couple of years rather than struggle for the rest of our lives.*
>
> Shaun, 19 - Troy, 2 months

A too-early pregnancy is likely to upset the parents of both the teenagers involved. Shaun's parents' support meant he could continue his college education.

Dad's Role During Pregnancy

Financial support isn't the only thing a father can contribute. When a couple is together during pregnancy, whether or not they live together, dad can play an important role in helping her have a healthy pregnancy. After all, it's his baby too.

If your girlfriend or wife is pregnant, you can encourage her to eat the foods she and your baby need.

When she was pregnant, I used to cook for her. I'd fix her eggs in the morning, and I'd make salads for her. I never used to like cooking, but when she got pregnant, I started saying, "She's got to get some food inside that baby."

Manuel

Statistically, teenage mothers are more likely to deliver babies who are too small and born too soon for good health. If the mother eats the foods she and her baby need throughout pregnancy, if she stays away from alcohol, cigarettes, and drugs, and if she sees her doctor regularly, she probably will have a healthy baby. You can help her do so.

When Bethann was pregnant I'd get on her case to see that she ate right and got to the doctor. I was like a watchdog for her. I was very upset that she quit going to school. I'd like her out of school as soon as possible. Her high school diploma is very important, and I think she agrees.

Shaun

If you and your partner go out partying, she may be tempted by the alcohol and drugs. Perhaps you'll decide to help her by being a good example yourself. If you don't drink or take drugs, it will probably be easier for her not to give these things to your unborn child.

If the mother smokes, the unborn child suffers. In Chapter 5, Meghan explains how her boyfriend helped her quit smoking during her second pregnancy.

Even being in a smoke-filled room is hard on a fetus. If you smoke, you may choose to cut back, perhaps quit because of your baby. If not, perhaps you'll not smoke around your partner and unborn child.

Sharing Prenatal Care Visits

Are you able to go to the doctor with her for each prenatal health checkup? She would appreciate your support. It's also part of becoming close to your child even before s/he is born. Listening to your unborn baby's heartbeat through the doctor's Doptone (ultrasound stethoscope) is exciting. So is seeing the ultrasound, the "picture" the doctor may take of the fetus.

Randy and Whitney couldn't be together for several months during Whitney's pregnancy. He mentioned the ultrasound as making him feel a little more involved in the situation:

We both knew she was pregnant when I left, but Whitney didn't tell her parents until I came back. She was seven months then.

We wrote to each other during that time, and she sent me a couple of ultrasounds. That made the baby more real for me.

When Whitney was pregnant I was happy and scared at the same time. I was scared about what was going to happen, but happy about having him. I didn't walk out because we both agreed to have this baby, and I wanted to see my daughter or son. I didn't want the baby to suffer. That's why I didn't walk out on her. It's pretty scary though.

When I came back, Whitney was real grouchy. She stayed with her parents until Keegan was born. Then she moved in with me and my parents.

I graduate this year. I had planned to go to college, but now I'll have to get a job instead.

Randy, 17 - Keegan, 2 months

Your emotional support is probably the most important thing you can offer your partner right now. Whether the pregnancy is planned or unplanned, no matter what her age, most women experience hormonal changes that cause them to be easily upset during pregnancy.

In addition to these physical changes, your partner may have other problems. Her parents may be upset about the pregnancy. She may find it difficult to continue her education. The future may look pretty scary. Your support could help her cope with these feelings.

She Needs a Labor Coach

Thinking about her approaching labor and delivery may be frightening for your partner. Taking a prepared childbirth class together would help you both prepare for the important task of getting your baby born. At these classes, you'll learn how you can act as her "coach" for the big event.

If you are her labor coach, you'll encourage her to breathe in certain ways during her contractions and to focus on a specific point as she labors. Rubbing her back or simply letting her hold your hand tightly during her contractions will help. Prepared childbirth classes advise you of other ways you can be involved in the birth of your child.

Research shows a father who is with his partner when their baby is born is likely to be closer to the mother and baby a year later than are fathers who were not involved in their child's birth.

At first I didn't like her being pregnant because I was too young. Then after I saw her have the baby and they let me cut the cord, joy came to me. I got happy and tears started coming out of my eyes.
                              Leandro, 17 - Jonathan, 18 months

I was with her in the delivery room. I tripped out. When I first saw him coming out, when I saw his head, it was weird.

*I stayed at the hospital with them that night,
and we had the baby in the room with us. The nurse
taught us to sponge bathe him and not to get the
cord wet.*

*She showed us how to make bottles, how to clean
him and change him, and how to keep him wrapped
up. She kept coming in to ask if we needed help.*

Andy, 17 - Gus, 5 months

Sometimes fathers have jealous feelings after their baby
is born. Your partner may seem totally absorbed in the
baby and have no time left for you. Perhaps she seems
exhausted much of the time. Your best defense is to be as
involved as possible with her in caring for your child.

Taking Responsibility

Randy knew he needed to stay in school. Dropping out
and trying to support his family at a minimum pay job
didn't make sense. There were other ways he could be
responsible right now:

*Before delivery I took everything out of my room
that I didn't need so I could make space for the crib
and stroller and other things for the baby. Whitney
picked out the color, and I painted the room. Whitney
got lots of things at her baby shower, and that helped.*

Randy

Even if you can't offer much financial support right
now, you can be involved in the care of your child. Do your
share of baby care. Perhaps your parents can provide some
childcare.

If you're both in school, you may need to set up a schedule for childcare which will allow time for each of you to
do your home work.

Do you have health insurance? If so, check to see if it
covers your baby too.

It's Not Easy

Andy speaks for many teen fathers when he discusses the difficulties of having a child before he was ready:

> *The hard thing is you're still a kid and you can't deny it. There's nothing you can do about it. You got yourself into this mess. I wish I had never had kids because there are a lot of things I'd like to be doing now. But you can't change what you've done. You have to deal with it even though there are times when you say, "This sucks." You see a lot of your friends who don't have kids, and you wish you were like them.*
>
> *Now I have to think about my baby when I'm walking on the street, and it feels weird. Before, I didn't have anyone to think about except myself. Now I have to watch out for all three of us. I was mostly raised to take care of myself. I understood there wouldn't be anybody there to help me out.*
>
> *Now I have to think of them. It's hard.*
>
> Andy

Of course it's hard. Parenting a child is one of the most difficult—*and* one of the most rewarding—tasks faced by human beings. Getting pregnant before she's ready changes a young woman's life tremendously. It also drastically changes her baby's father's life.

Teen fathers who hang in there, who choose to face the great responsibility of supporting and actively parenting their child, may face hardship and broken dreams just as their baby's mother does. When you choose this route, you also can look forward to the joys of seeing your baby grow, first into a charming and independent toddler, then through childhood and on to becoming the responsible, mature adult you want him to be.

What a wonderful challenge!

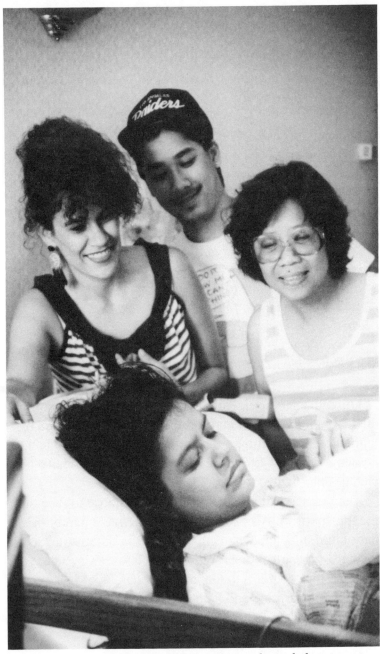

They're all concerned about you and your baby.

CHAPTER 13

THREE-GENERATION LIVING

Teenage parents, married as well as single, are more likely to live with their parents than is an older family. How does this change their approach to baby care and child rearing?

The following dialog is typical of the young families interviewed:

Andrea (17): *I take most of the responsibility—it's the way it works. They all (sisters, mother) drop little helpful hints, but that's about it. I can ignore those.*

Grandmother: *At first it was hard because I wanted to hold him. But I tried not to be too over-bearing because I didn't want to upset Andrea.*

Ted (baby's father)**:** *Look at the pictures—you're in every one of them!*

Grandmother: *I couldn't wait to get him home.*

Andrea: *Everything upset me that first week. It upset me that Mom took Dennis and was running around the house showing him off.*

Grandmother: *He was the most beautiful baby in the entire hospital.*

Andrea: *Mom with the baby and Ted with the camera—that was the first day. I was upset. But I was kind of glad she took him for awhile so I could sleep.*

Andrea, 16, and Ted, 18 - Dennis, 2 months

Help from Grandma

On the positive side, it is often reassuring as well as less tiring to have some help with baby care. New parents may suddenly feel they don't know how to take care of this small creature.

When I came home from the hospital, sometimes I'd feel really scared. I didn't know what to do. I was even scared to carry Racquelle. When she cried and cried, I cried myself because I didn't know what was wrong.

Cheryl, 15 - Racquelle, 2 months

I could baby-sit easily, but when it came to my baby, I needed my mom. She was too bossy, but I did need her.

I'm a new mother and I need help. But I have my own instincts, and I think I know what is best. She thinks her way is much better because she's older and a nurse. But I'm a mother too, and I think I should try my way to see if it works.

If I were living on my own, I think I'd be a nervous wreck. I wouldn't have anyone to ask for advice. But there are times when I want to try something myself because I want to be the responsible person.

Holly, 17 - Orlando, 5 months

Having your mother in the same house can be reassuring. During the early weeks of night feeding, she may even be willing to take an occasional turn at getting up with the baby while you sleep.

> *She loves me and she loves the baby, but the baby*
> *is my responsibility. A couple of times Sonja would*
> *wake up at night and cry and cry. I would cry, too,*
> *and Mom would come in and help. But I want Sonja*
> *to know me as her mother.*
>
> Julie, 16 - Sonja, 7 months

"Who's My Mother?"

The neat thing about grandmas is that they're experienced. They've learned from their mistakes. They take time, and have learned how to be patient with a fussy baby.

The not-so-good news is that sometimes grandparents take on too much responsibility. They may appear to forget who the mom is.

If grandmother takes over in the beginning, it may be hard for baby's own mother to take charge later. The result in many families is a baby who thinks grandma is her mother. Baby's mother then feels left out and resentful. Most hurt may be baby who isn't sure who mother really is.

> *I've caught my mother a few times playing the*
> *mother role. I can understand that because she has*
> *the experience. Besides, I really need that when I'm*
> *tired or don't feel good. But other times I don't like it.*
> *I'll be playing with Karl, and she'll come in and pick*
> *him up and take him off with her. I don't like that*
> *at all.*
>
> *I take Karl with me everywhere I can, and my*
> *mother is constantly telling me I shouldn't do that,*
> *that I'm not being fair to Karl. But if I had to stay*

*home all the time with him, I'd be miserable. And if
I'm miserable, so is Karl. I think it's all right. He's
seeing new things, being with people. He's learning
more from going places with me.*

*Sometimes I have to explain to my mom that I have
taken on this responsibility of being a mother, and I
want to do it the whole way. I know when Karl is
hungry, when he needs a bath, etc., but my mom still
tries to tell me to do all these things. I try not to let it
bother me—but it does.*

*Because I'm underage, it would be hard to live
alone. I wouldn't have anybody around when I'm
sick. I wouldn't have anybody to talk to—and I
couldn't afford a place of my own.*

                                    Kimberly, 17 - Karl, 2 months

Role of Brothers and Sisters

If you have brothers and/or sisters living with you, you'll
need to consider their feelings too. Will their lives change
much because of your baby? Will they be expected to do
more of the housework because you'll be so busy with
your child?

How do you think they'll feel about that? There probably
is no "right" answer, but it's a topic you and your family
should consider *before your baby arrives.*

*Sometimes my sisters want to give me advice. I let
them say what they want. I can ignore them.*

*For example, just lately Stevie gets crabby when
he's having a bowel movement. When they see him
fussing, they tell me to feed him. Or they think I
should "do" something.*

*When he was just two weeks old, they wanted to
shake rattles in his face. He didn't want that. He's
just a little baby. I'd tell them that, and they'd go
running to tell my mom, "Alison doesn't want us to do*

*anything with her baby." My mom would laugh and
tell them I know what I'm doing. I think my sisters get
annoyed at my being here all the time with the baby.
But when I ask them to baby-sit so I can go out for a
little while, they usually refuse.*

Alison, 18 - Stevie 3 months

Key—Take Responsibility Yourself

Beth realizes how important it is to take care of her
baby herself:

*I really can't go anywhere now, especially since
I'm breastfeeding. I'm limited in the things I do, even
though I have my mother around. She loves taking
care of Patty, but I don't want to become dependent
on her. I want to take the responsibility. That's where
my older sister kind of messed up. She depended on
my mom to take care of the baby whenever she
wanted to go someplace, and I don't want that to
happen. It's nice having Mom around.*

Beth, 18 - Patty, 3 weeks

Cheryl has also seen the problems in letting her mother
take over:

*I thought it would be my mom taking care of
Racquelle all the time. With my two sisters who got
pregnant at 16, she took over. They didn't know
anything about taking care of their babies.*

*When I brought Racquelle home, I took care of her
by myself all the time. I showed my mom I could do it.
Now that she knows she doesn't have to take care of
her, she'll baby-sit sometimes when I want to go out.*

Cheryl

If a young mother doesn't want grandma to take charge,
the secret seems to be in showing that she is indeed capable
of caring for her own child. Alison's mother explained:

Alison does everything. If I weren't working it would be harder not to take over. I'm surprised at myself that I haven't done that. That was a concern I had when she was pregnant. I knew this had to be her baby, her responsibility.

I love babies, and I like to take care of them, but I've not gotten up even once with Stevie. In fact, I don't hear him cry at night!

Her daughter added:

Stevie's such a good baby, but I do think I have to keep him quiet. Dad can take quite a bit, but I know he doesn't like to hear babies cry. It would be a lot harder if he were a fussy baby. Then I think my family might get irritated. But since he sleeps in my room, I just pick him up and nurse him when he wakes up at night. He goes right back to sleep.

If you're a young parent living with your parents, you may feel you have no choice. You probably also appreciate their help very much.

An extended family of baby, mother, and/or father, and grandparents at its best means more love and TLC (Tender Loving Care) for baby—and that's great!

Sometimes the relationship between a teen mom and her mother even improves after the baby is born:

My relationship with my mom became a little better because I started thinking about my kids and how I wanted my kids to treat me. And I started thinking of her as a friend as well as a mother.

Mom really really respects me in my motherhood. She asks to hold the baby, and that makes me feel good. She doesn't act like I'm just a little kid trying to raise a baby.

Kellie, 16 - Kevin, 3 months

Will Everyone Agree?

With more people in the house, there will be more interacting—more people who may wake up when baby cries, and more people who resent the mess of wet diapers and other baby things around.

With more people, there will be more disagreement, too, as to whether baby needs to be picked up when she cries, or whether she is simply trying to get to sleep. "Don't pick her up, you'll spoil her" can be fighting words if it's grandma talking to a young mother who is convinced that a newborn's crying means something is wrong.

> *My mom is good, and she helps me a lot, but on some things I disagree with her. I don't think you can spoil a newborn baby, and I feel strongly about that. She needs all the loving she can get.*
>
> *My mom tells me I shouldn't pick Patty up when she cries, but I won't let her cry very long. I say times change, she raised five, but I know some things, too.*

Beth

Your best defense is education. Learn how and why things happen to baby. Your informed responses to suggestions from others are great tools.

If you and/or your parents would like to read about other "three-generation" families made up of a teenage daughter (or son), her/his baby, and the teenager's parent(s), see *School-Age Parents: The Challenge of Three-Generation Living* (Morning Glory Press: 1990). Reading *School-Age Parents* together might help you and your parents understand each other and each other's needs a little better.

Three generations—baby, parents, and grandparents—living in the same house or apartment means everyone must give a little, sometimes a lot. When you get uptight, try to remember that all that extra love can be a real advantage for your baby.

Delaying the second pregnancy means more time and attention for your first baby—and a greater chance to reach your own goals.

CHAPTER 14

ANOTHER BABY— WHEN?

Many teen mothers get pregnant again soon after the birth of their first child. In fact, more than half are pregnant within two years after their first delivery.

Is this what you want? Or would you rather wait a while longer before getting pregnant again? Reasons you might like to wait include:

- Being able to give your first child the attention and care s/he needs. Toddlers need as much attention, although of a different kind, as infants.

- With one child, you may be able to find child care so you can continue school and work toward your other goals. With two children, it would be much harder.

- More babies usually mean more poverty.

- Your body is less likely to produce a healthy baby if your pregnancies are too close together.

- Your relationship with your partner is likely to suffer if you have too many children in too short a time.

If you would prefer to delay your next pregnancy, are you planning now how you'll achieve that goal?

Of course no one *has* to be sexually active. Abstinence from sexual activity permits the couple to explore their relationship in many other ways.

Abstinence: Not having sexual intercourse

Sex Often Changes Relationship

Sexual activity is both physical and emotional. The emotional part of sexual intercourse may be quite different for each partner.

Sometimes one partner holds the power in a relationship because the other person has such strong emotions concerning the sexual act. This power can have an important effect on the relationship.

Generally, neither partner feels the same after they begin having sexual intercourse. That can be good, or it can cause serious differences between the two. Pregnancy further complicates things.

During pregnancy is a good time to think about family planning. You can't get pregnant again quite yet, so you have time to look at your options with little risk.

Issues to Consider

Several issues are involved in contraceptive decision-making:

- Some people think the young woman who "takes precautions" is not a "nice girl."

- A woman who has been in an unhappy relationship may truly feel she'll never be in a sexual relationship again.

- Women often feel the contraceptive decision should be made between partners.

First, the "nice girl" issue. If she isn't ready to have a baby, not getting pregnant is a responsible approach, an approach that appears mature and caring. Aren't nice girls mature and caring?

A woman who carries condoms with her is showing her partner that she cares about herself, her future, and his. That's being a nice girl.

Second, the teen who doesn't plan ever to have sexual intercourse again may be sincere. However, a teenager has about thirty years of fertility left. She is likely to need family planning information at some time during those years.

Third, the issue of the partners deciding together. The fact is that many couples find it extremely difficult to talk about sex at all. Discussing family planning at length is even harder.

Most of my friends, who are already teen moms, are afraid to say, "Use a condom" to their partners. They know about it, but the barrier is trying to talk to your partner. Sometimes they talk about it, and the partner says, "No, I won't use it." Then they give up. I think they need to take care of themselves because of the babies they have now.

Angelica, pregnant at 17

Some young women say their partners don't want them to use birth control. One student even told us her boyfriend wouldn't "let" her use birth control because he thought if she did, she might have sex with other guys. A relationship with so little trust between the partners appears to be in trouble. If she's going to continue to have sex with this boyfriend, this young woman might decide to use a contraceptive in spite of his objections. Christina agrees:

I've told my boyfriend I don't want to get pregnant again, and that I'm going to take care of myself.

Christina, pregnant at 15

Other Objections to Contraception

Other objections to using contraception include:

- "I can't afford it." (Babies cost more than contraception.)

- "I don't have transportation to the clinic." (Keeping your prenatal care appointments takes transportation too.)

- My mother might find out. (Your mother will notice when you're eight months pregnant.)

The person who can get pregnant surely should have the right to decide whether she wants to be pregnant or not. If she doesn't, she needs either to abstain from sex or use an effective contraceptive.

The doctor will usually discuss birth control with you at your postpartum check-up. Be sure you keep this appointment, and be prepared with questions.

Remember, the medical staff is not there to judge you or anyone else. They will be happy to give you information and assistance. It's their job, and they like to think their work counts. They probably feel strongly that planned children are preferable.

Lots of Options

There is a wide variety of contraceptive devices. Each person needs to consider what's available, then decide which is best for her/him.

Types of Contraceptives

Barriers: Condom, diaphragm, sponge and cervical cap

Spermicides: Jelly, foam, suppositories

Systemics: Birth control pills; implants

IUD: The intrauterine device

Several contraceptives do not require a prescription, and you can buy them in almost any drugstore. These include spermicidal jelly or foam, the condom, cervical sponge, and suppositories. All of them kill sperm or prevent them from getting into the uterus.

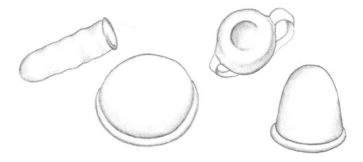

Condom, diaphragm, sponge, and cervical cap

These methods also help prevent the spread of sexually transmitted diseases (STDs). The condom does this best, but the other products kill some germs.

The man needs to put the condom on carefully *before* he has any sexual contact with his partner. It will feel more comfortable and be less likely to break if he leaves one-half inch of space at the end as he rolls it on his erect penis.

The diaphragm is a molded rubber cup that is placed in the vagina to keep the sperm from getting into the uterus. You need to see a doctor to be fitted for a diaphragm.

The diaphragm is used with a special spermicidal jelly. This method of birth control has no side effects. It can be placed in the vagina up to several hours before sexual contact. Add more jelly before each sexual contact.

Important: The diaphragm, to be effective, needs to be left in the vagina six to eight hours after intercourse.

The cervical cap is similar to the diaphragm, but it can be left in for eight to forty-eight hours.

The sponge is also similar to the diaphragm, but it can only be used once. The medicine in the sponge can be irritating to some people's skin.

Suppositories are small wax-like pellets that are placed in the vagina before sexual contact. They melt at body temperature, releasing a sperm-killing substance. A suppository contraceptive is effective for about six hours.

Spermicides

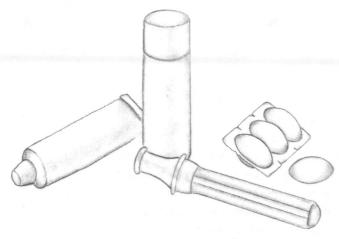

Contraceptive jelly, foam, and suppositories

Items such as the condom, foam, and jelly are sometimes available free at your local health department. The effects of foam and jelly are temporary. They must be used at or near the time of sexual contact.

Birth Control Pill

Birth control pills are widely available from doctors and clinics. Insurance or Medicaid often pays for this service. The advantage of the pill is that it doesn't have to be used at the time of sexual intercourse. You do have to be sure you take one every day.

Birth control pill

If you don't have someone there to remind you, you can forget about it. Tyson reminds me. We never talked about birth control before I got pregnant. I didn't think it would happen to me—but it did.

Frederica, 16 - Jesse, 5 months

Some people delay their second pregnancy because they want more time with their first child.

The pill is available in different doses. Even if you've taken it before and you weren't happy with it, talk with your doctor again. S/he might suggest a different dosage for you.

Usually a person gets a two- to twelve-month supply of the pill. Some women have mild side effects after they start taking this contraceptive. These side effects seldom last any longer than a couple of months.

Note: The pill will not keep you from getting pregnant the first month you take it. Use another contraceptive during that month if you're sexually active.

Taking the pill may cut back on a breastfeeding mother's supply of milk. If you're breastfeeding, talk to your doctor. Some pills have little effect on the production of breast milk. You might prefer to use another contraceptive while you're breastfeeding.

Intrauterine Device (IUD)

The IUD (Intrauterine Device) is a plastic device about an inch long that is placed in the uterus by the doctor during a pelvic examination. Once there, it stays in for several years. (The IUD comes in various shapes.)

The IUD is recommended only for women who have had a child and who are in a sexual relationship with only one person. The risk of infection from the IUD increases if the person has several partners.

IUD

Contraceptive Implant

The newest family planning device is the implant. It is a low dose of birth control medicine in a capsule. The capsule is placed by a doctor under the skin of the patient's upper arm. (It doesn't show.) Once there, it slowly releases the pregnancy-preventing medicine for at least one year. Some types of implant may

Contraceptive implant

prevent pregnancy for up to five years. The implant is new on the market, and the cost may be covered by insurance.

A birth control hormone injection for guys may be available in a year or two. The injection will keep sperm from forming for one week. For effective birth control, the man would need to have an injection each week.

If you don't want to be pregnant again soon, make plans to prevent pregnancy. Choose not to have sex or, if you're having sex, use birth control—always.

STD Concerns

Sexually active people also need to be concerned about sexually transmitted diseases (STDs). Some of these conditions, such as a yeast infection, are merely annoying. Others have much more long-lasting effects and need immediate treatment. AIDS causes death.

Using a condom prevents the transmission of these diseases. It's even better if a spermicidal jelly is used with the condom. Remember that, as far as STDs are concerned, when you have sexual intercourse, you're having sex with everyone with whom your partner has ever had sex. If your partner caught an STD from a former partner, s/he can give you the disease.

If you ever have any of the following symptoms, even if you haven't had sexual intercourse for awhile, see your doctor or go to a clinic:

- Painful urination (both men and women)
- Unusual discharge from the penis or vagina
- Sore or itching genitals (sex organs)
- Lumps or growths around genital areas
- Rashes or blisters on the genital area
- Sores on the penis, on the vulva, or in the vagina

Vulva: Female outside sex area

Remember: Most sexually transmitted diseases can be treated without serious lifelong effects if you see the doctor soon enough. Medicaid and private insurance pay for this type of care. Public health departments are especially good at providing free or very low cost treatment for STDs.

AIDS—The Incurable STD

The one exception to that statement about successful treatment is AIDS. AIDS stands for Acquired Immune Deficiency Syndrome. The AIDS virus makes the body unable to resist diseases. A person with AIDS could die from any disease, but usually cancer or pneumonia is the cause of death.

There are no early symptoms *and no cure* for this disease. People who have AIDS can be given care for the symptoms and should receive that care. However, they will not be cured. In the past some people have gotten AIDS through blood transfusions, but this is almost impossible today because of improved testing of blood.

Today people get AIDS by:

- Having sex with an infected person

- Sharing needles or syringes with infected people who use any intravenous drugs
- Having sex with someone who shares needles with IV drug users
- Before birth from his/her mother

Caring for Yourself and Your Family

Remember that the more partners you have, the more likely you are to get a sexually transmitted disease. Think about other ways to have a loving relationship. Delay sex until you know your partner well. Discuss protection from pregnancy before you begin the sexual part of the relationship. Consider the risks that both pregnancy and sexually transmitted disease may present to you and your partner.

About half of all couples who have unprotected intercourse a dozen times will become pregnant.

Having your next child when you and your partner are physically, emotionally, and financially ready is better for your present child and your future family. It's up to you and your partner to make this happen. And if your partner isn't interested, *it's up to you.*

Appendix

About the Authors

Jean Brunelli, PHN, has worked with hundreds of pregnant teenagers. For fifteen years she has been teaching

prenatal health and parenting in the Teen Mother Program, ABC Unified School District, Cerritos, California.

A school nurse, she is also the director of the Handicapped Infant Program at the same school.

Jean is a graduate of Mt. St. Mary's College, Los Angeles. She and Mike have two grown children.

Jeanne Warren Lindsay is the author of twelve other books dealing with adolescent pregnancy and parenting. She, too, has worked with hundreds of pregnant and parenting teenagers. She developed the Teen Mother Program at Tracy High School, Cerritos, in 1972, and continues as a consultant in the program.

She has completed graduate degrees in Anthropology and Home Economics. She and Bob have five grown children and five grandchildren.

Bibliography

Arthur, Shirley. *Surviving Teen Pregnancy: Your Choices, Dreams and Decisions*. 1991. 192 pp. Morning Glory Press, 6595 San Haroldo Way, Buena Park, CA 90620.

> Helps pregnant teens understand their alternatives. Offers guidance in learning the art of decision-making.

Barr, Linda, and Catherine Monserrat. *Teenage Pregnancy: A New Beginning*. 1991. New Futures, Inc., 5400 Cutler, NE, Albuquerque, NM 87110.

> Prenatal health book written specifically for pregnant adolescents.

Becker, Kayla M., with Connie K. Heckert. *To Keera with Love*. 1987. Sheed and Ward, Kansas City, MO. Also available from Morning Glory Press

> Dramatic true story of Kayla's too-early pregnancy and the adoption plan she made for her beloved daughter.

Brinkley, Ginny, and Sherry Sampson. *Young and Pregnant—A Book For You.* 1989. 73 pp. Pink Inc! 8230-I Baycenter Road, Jacksonville, FL 32256. $3.95.
Refreshingly simple book on prenatal care directed to teenagers. Provides basic information.

Lindsay, Jeanne Warren, and Jean Brunelli. Translation by Argentina Palacios. *Adolocentes como padres—La jornada de tu embarazo y el nacimiento de tu bebé.* 1993. 192 pp. Morning Glory Press, 6595 San Haroldo, Buena Park, CA 90620. Paper, $9.95; Cloth, $15.95. Workbook., $2.50; Teacher's Guide, $2.50.
Teens Parenting—Your Pregnancy and Newborn Journey is also available in Spanish to meet the needs of Spanish-speaking teens and their parents.

Lindsay, Jeanne Warren. *Do I Have a Daddy? A Story About a Single-Parent Child.* 1991. 48 pp. Morning Glory Press. Paper, $5.95; Cloth, $12.95.
A beautiful book for the child who has never met his/her father. A special sixteen-page section offers suggestions to single mothers.

_____. *Pregnant Too Soon: Adoption Is an Option.* 1988. Morning Glory Press.
Young women who were, by their own admission, "pregnant too soon," speak for themselves. They share their reasons for making the tremendously difficult decision to release their baby for adoption. Also includes information on father's rights and other legal aspects of adoption.

_____. *Open Adoption: A Caring Option.* 1987. Morning Glory Press. 256 pp. $9.95; $15.95.
Sensitive account of the new world of open adoption. Many quotes. Relates experiences of birthparents choosing adoptive parents for their baby and adoptive parents maintaining contact with their baby's birthparents.

_____. *Parents, Pregnant Teens and the Adoption Option: Help for Families*. 1989. 208 pp. Morning Glory Press.

Guidance for parents of pregnant teenagers considering an adoption plan.

_____. *School-Age Parents: The Challenge of Three-Generation Living*. 1990. 224 pp. Morning Glory Press.

A much needed book for dealing with the frustrations, problems, and pleasures of three-generation living.

_____. *Teenage Marriage: Coping with Reality*. 1988. 208 pp. Morning Glory Press.

Marriage book written especially for teenagers. Based on in-depth interviews with married teens and on nationwide survey of more than 3000 teenagers' attitudes toward marriage.

_____. *Teens Parenting—Your Baby's First Year. Teens Parenting—The Challenge of Toddlers*. 1991. 192 pp. each. Morning Glory Press.

Two how-to-parent books especially for teenage parents.

_____ and Sally McCullough. *Teens Parenting—Discipline from Birth to Three*. 1991. 192 pp. Morning Glory Press.

Provides teenage parents with guidelines to help prevent discipline problems with their children and guidelines for dealing with problems when they occur.

Peterson, Judy. *Inside-Outside*. Published quarterly. 16 pp. Inside-Outside, 4680 Lake Underhill, Orlando, FL 32807.

Beautiful full-color quarterly magazine for teenage parents. Lots of photos. Good information very simply and interestingly written. Shows respect for teenage parents.

Parent Express Series. ANR Publications, University of
   California, 6701 San Pablo Avenue, Oakland, CA
   94608-1239.

   Wonderful series of newsletters for parents. The first set starts
   two months before delivery and continues through the first
   year of the child's life. Second set covers second and third
   years.

Renfrew, Mary, Chloe Fisher, Suzanne Arms. *Bestfeeding:
   Getting Breastfeeding Right for You.* 1990. 225 pp.
   Celestial Arts Publishing, P.O. Box 7327, Berkeley,
   CA 94707.
   Good description, with lots of photographs and drawings, of
   the importance of breastfeeding and of how to make the
   process work.

Schnell, Barry T. *The Teenage Parent's Support Guide.*
   1989. 135 pp. The Advocacy Center for Child
   Support, P.O. 276, Yorklyn, DE 19736.

   For teenage parents, a guide to their basic rights and
   obligations and to legal procedures.

Silverstein, Herma. *Teenage and Pregnant: What You
   Can Do.* 1988. 154 pp. Julian Messner, Simon &
   Schuster, Inc., Prentice Hall Building, Englewood
   Cliffs, NJ 07632. 154 pp.

   Well-written non-judgmental discussion of the issues facing
   pregnant teenagers.

Simkin, Penny. Drawings by Marianne Brorup. "Cami Has
   a Baby." 1990. 16 pp. Pennypress, Inc., 1100 23rd
   Avenue East, Seattle, WA 98112.

   A comic book for pregnant teenagers provides honest look at a
   teen mother's experience of pregnancy, childbirth, and early
   parenthood.

Index

BOOKS FROM MORNING GLORY PRESS

TEENS PARENTING—Your Pregnancy and Newborn Journey
Available in "regular" (RL 6), Easier Reading (RL 3), and Spanish.

Described in Bibliography:

TEENS PARENTING—Your Baby's First Year

TEENS PARENTING—The Challenge of Toddlers

TEENS PARENTING—Discipline from Birth to Three

Workbooks for above titles + following guides:

You Can Help Pregnant and Parenting Teens, Book 1: Teacher's Guide for Teens Parenting Series. Answer key for four workbooks.

You Can Help Pregnant and Parenting Teens, Book 2: Curriculum Guide for Teens Parenting Series.

TEEN DADS: Rights, Responsibilities and Joys by Jeanne Lindsay
Parenting book especially for teenage fathers. Workbook, Teacher's Guide.

DETOUR FOR EMMY by Marilyn Reynolds
Young adult novel about Emmy, pregnant and 15. Wonderful supplementary title to use with *Teens Parenting* series.

TEENS LOOK AT MARRIAGE: Rainbows, Roles and Reality
Describes the research behind *Teenage Marriage.*

ADOPTION AWARENESS: A Guide for Teachers, Nurses, Counselors and Caring Others
Guide for supporting adoption alternative in crisis pregnancy.

BREAKING FREE FROM PARTNER ABUSE for teenage and other victims of domestic violence. Underlying theme, "You don't deserve this!"

TEEN PREGNANCY CHALLENGE, Book One: Strategies for Change; Book Two: Programs for Kids
Book One provides practical guidelines for developing adolescent pregnancy prevention and care programs. *Book Two* focuses on programs all along the adolescent pregnancy prevention continuum.

Please see other titles in Annotated Bibliography.

Please see ordering information on back of page.

MORNING GLORY PRESS

6595 San Haroldo Way, Buena Park, CA 90620
714/828-1998 — FAX 714/828-2049

See catalog for workbook, curriculum guide information on following books.

Please send me the following:	Price	Total
Teens Parenting—Your Pregnancy and Newborn Journey		
___Paper, ISBN 0-930934-50-4	9.95	_____
Easier Reading Edition—*Your Pregnancy and Newborn Journey*		
___Paper, ISBN 0-930934-61-x	9.95	_____
Spanish—**Adolescentes como padres**—La jornada de tu embarazo y el nacimiento de tu bebé		
___Paper, ISBN 0-930934-69-5	9.95	_____
Teens Parenting—Your Baby's First Year		
___Paper, ISBN 0-930934-52-0	9.95	_____
Teens Parenting—Challenge of Toddlers		
___Paper, ISBN 0-930934-58-x	9.95	_____
Teens Parenting—Discipline from Birth to Three		
___Paper, ISBN 0-930934-54-7	9.95	_____
Surviving Teen Pregnancy		
___Paper, ISBN 0-930934-47-4	9.95	_____
Teen Dads: Rights, Responsibilities and Joys		
___Paper, ISBN 0-930934-78-4	9.95	_____
Detour for Emmy		
___Paper, ISBN 0-930934-76-8	8.95	_____
School-Age Parents: Coping with Three-Generation Living		
___Paper, ISBN 0-930934-36-9	10.95	_____
Breaking Free from Partner Abuse		
___Paper, ISBN 0-930934-74-1	7.95	_____
Teen Pregnancy Challenge,		
___*Book 1: Strategies for Change*	14.95	_____
___*Book 2: Programs for Kids*	14.95	_____
___*Pregnant Too Soon: Adoption Is an Option*	9.95	_____
___*Open Adoption: A Caring Option*	9.95	_____
___*Adoption Awareness:*	12.95	_____
___*Parents, Pregnant Teens and Adoption Option*	8.95	_____
___*Teenage Marriage: Coping with Reality*	9.95	_____
___*Teens Look at Marriage*	9.95	_____
___*Do I Have a Daddy?*	5.95	_____
	TOTAL	_____
Please add postage: 10% of total—Min., $2.50		_____
California residents add 7.75% sales tax		_____
	TOTAL	_____

Ask about quantity discounts, Teacher, Student Guides.
Prepayment requested. School/library purchase orders accepted.
If not satisfied, return in 15 days for refund.

NAME _____

ADDRESS _____

_____